Ellin Randel

A Secret Core of Joy

A SECRET CORE OF JOY

BY

ELLIN RANDEL

Small Batch Books
Amherst, Massachusetts

Cover image: Ellin Randel at twelve
Frontispiece: childhood drawing by Ellin Randel

ISBN 978-0-9829758-0-0
Library of Congress Control Number 2010938028

SMALL
BATCH
BOOKS

493 South Pleasant Street
Amherst, Massachusetts 01002
413.230.3943
SMALLBATCHBOOKS.COM

To my Guru,
Swami Muktananda

Flo

I was born on a cold day in February
In the middle of the Depression
To a Mother who loved me not
A love knot knotted her love
It wood knot Flo
And so
I died
Not dead but
Knot alive
Nobody knew my name
So they named me Ellin
Meaning Light
A good start
To a bad beginning
From there I went nowhere as fast as I could
And ended up here
Having come a long way
Through the cold February of my life
Through the Great Depression of my life
To the love knot of my life-death
To the Light

ᴄ꙰ Contents

ca PROLOGUE

Lives

THERE THEY WERE, LIKE CLOTHES hanging in a closet, and I shuffled through them—a rag-tag collection of old karmic debts, some shiny, some worn at the sleeves and tired-looking. I was here to choose one—my next life. I must have looked at them and thought, "Oh, let's just finish them all off—there aren't so many." And so I ended up with this rag-tag life, with so many different parts to it, it's hard to fit them all together and make one puzzle with the result.

There are parts of me that I have not revisited in almost forty years, since the ending of my spectacularly successful psychoanalysis. Today, in my seventies, I allow myself to remember that when I was young, not a day went by that I did not long for death. When I grew old enough, into my teens, I longed to kill myself. I thought about it constantly, but had little imagination for how I would do it. My most convincing image was of stabbing myself with a knife, since that was at least available. Guns were not. Pills were not. Stabbing myself was a constant theme, and it elaborated eventually into an even more powerful and persistent image. My image of life was one of holding a huge sack—almost as big as me—of razor blades. I stood and hugged it to me in my vision, and that described the way I experienced my life. These images manifested in my outer life, eventually. I have had more than my share of surgeries, minor and major. The knives I created in the depths of my unconscious found a way to live.

Gradually, in the course of my six-year psychoanalysis, I got over the desire to die, or rather to be dead. But looking back on that time, and remembering the intensity of my feelings, I realize that two (at least) things still linger from it. One is paralysis. I am strikingly paralyzed when it comes to manifesting my own creative energies. I have stacks of poems and other writings, books full of drawings, walls of paintings and pastels and other art work I've done. They come from my conscious mind but up until now I didn't even notice, and certainly didn't reflect on, the unconscious content of them.

But I've never sent anything out into the world. One reason is: *I don't know how.* Another is: *that part of me is paralyzed.* What strikes me now, first, is that the paralysis I speak of is like the muscle paralysis that occurs during dreaming—it protects you from acting out the images of the dream. I think of the paralysis as a disability, but it may also be the thing that kept me alive all those years. The thought *I don't know how* has the same potential—to protect me from myself. Like many artists and writers, I might have died from actively displaying the products of my creative energies, and thus finding that I could act, and I did know how.

One of the wonderful benefits of psychoanalysis is that as you discover, or uncover, the hidden parts of yourself, the things you have come to think of as your worst faults or glaring weaknesses turn out to have an emotional logic so powerful that you cannot but appreciate them. I might have died of showing my art or publishing my writing. That may be fantasy, but it may be true. Many artists have died relatively young, maybe of their art. I chose living over fulfilling my artistic dreams. Looking at it now, I'm not sorry.

ᛒ ONE
My Parents

WHEN MY MOTHER WAS A GIRL in the Bronx, in the teens and twenties, there were farms within walking distance of where she lived. It's one of the few things she told me about her childhood. Flo was the sixth of seven children. I don't have much of a picture of what life was like in her household. I know that my grandmother Ida was a seamstress— a dress designer, really, but we didn't refer to her as that. My mother still had a dress her mother had made for her to wear to a dance. It was a flapper dress, a totally magical garment fit for a fairy-tale princess. It was made of cobweb-soft pink silk, and my grandmother had hand-sewn silver sequins and bugle-beads in a design both front and back, and sewn a long bugle-bead fringe at the bottom of the dress. When my mother held it up to show it to me it hissed delicately as the fringe undulated. I still have the dress, torn and worn but still magnificent, in a box in the back of my closet.

My grandfather Morris owned a restaurant in downtown Manhattan. He had run a successful restaurant on the Lower East Side of Manhattan patronized, I was often told, by the Grand Street Boys. I had no idea who the Grand Street Boys were, but I do have a hazy notion that they were a political group. I imagine them as burly, cigar-smoking pols, wheeling and dealing and throwing their weight around downtown. My mother told me that my grandfather had left Russia when he was a young man, to avoid conscription into the army—something I found out years later was a horrible fate for Jews, who were treated badly and conscripted for life. My mother told me one other thing about her father: When she graduated from high school, she asked him for money to buy a class ring, "and he threw me down the stairs."

Another legend passed on to me was the story I heard many times, of my grandmother trying to call one of her children and having to go through the list—Abe, Joe, Jenny, Sue, Bea—till she got to the right name. I thought it was because she had so many children, but now I frequently find myself calling my grandson by my son's name, and I have revised my interpretation.

My mother was a good student, and was pretty and popular. When she graduated from high school she got a job as a Spanish interpreter/stenographer at an importing company. She was proud of her prowess at Spanish, though I never heard her speak it.

My grandparents' apartment had a long entrance hall with a glass-fronted cabinet at the end. In it, my grandmother kept her treasures, which held little interest for me until years later, when her Chinese ginger jar became mine, and I saw it was incredibly beautiful. Also in this room was a high chair, which was used by all the grandchildren when they came to visit. I remember my grandfather once trying to convince me to eat chocolate pudding as I sat in the high chair. He was sitting in front of me making yum-yum noises and I was stubbornly refusing to eat, because the pudding had a skin on it. It's the only face-to-face personal encounter I can recall having with my grandfather.

He was an imposing man, not tall but strongly built and with a thick head of silver hair and a bristly silver moustache. By the time I was born, my grandfather no longer owned his restaurant—why, I don't know. Now he bred canaries, which were in cages all over the apartment and sang loudly and constantly.

❧

I remember my father's mother as a tiny, shrunken, and wrinkled old woman who spoke not one word of English. When she came to visit us, about twice a year, she slept in my room. She muttered to herself and sang whiny songs in Yiddish. Most impressive to me, she wore a wig. The wig was brown and thick, and pulled back in a bun, an incongruous frame for her wizened face. I only knew it was a wig because she took it off at night, revealing her almost-bald head, a few wispy gray hairs wrapped in a cloth band. I see her in my mind's eye holding her wig, as distant and strange as a scene from a movie. The one connection we had was that when she visited she brought a large cardboard box full of little old used toys she had been gathering since her last visit. Things like little balls, cars, toy animals and people, little glass perfume bottles—the box was full, and it was an adventure to rummage through them—the most toys I'd ever seen at one time.

My father was about seven years older than my mother. Murray was handsome and had dark wavy hair and a sweet smile. He was already a businessman when they met. I think that impressed her. They hung out in a group of couples their age, and kept those friendships for the rest of their lives. The children of their friends became friends for my brother and me, and we addressed their parents as aunt and uncle.

My father's father died when my father was eleven, and he left school and went to work to help support his family. He never went to high school. He told me wistfully a few times of the struggle his mother had to care for her six children, how they often ate only beans. He also told me that when he was a kid a movie ticket was two for five cents. He would hang around the front of the theater waiting for another kid to come along with three cents, and he would chip in his two, and they'd buy a ticket. He often said longingly that his burning ambition had been to be the one with the three cents, but he never was. It marked him for life, actually. Whenever we went out in a group my father always insisted on paying for everyone. I think it filled some hole that was forever in him.

My mother had her own unfilled hole. I think love must have been scarce around her house when she was growing up. Not that her parents didn't love her—the dress my grandmother made for her is pure silk love. But there were so many brothers and sisters, and life was hard, and everyone had to work, and my mother, next to youngest, couldn't compete with her older, bigger, louder, handsome sisters. I know she projected a gigantic amount of self-doubt and anxiety onto me, and I can only imagine the deep wells in her that it came from, and the experiences that dug those wells.

My mother's approach to filling the hole inside was to stuff it with things. She craved fur coats and jewels. As my father's business grew and they approached prosperity, she accumulated mink coats and stoles, a fox stole, diamond pins and rings, gold bracelets, pearls, gold watches. Sometimes, when she wanted something new, she tossed one at me. I never knew what to do with these gifts. I can't remember taking pleasure in any of them.

When I was little my mother arrived at the level where she could hire a full-time, sleep-in maid. This meant that she was free to go out, and she did. I think she would have liked to go back to work, but my father wouldn't hear of it. In his mind, it cast doubt on his ability to take care of his family financially. (When I was a teenager he forbade me to take babysitting jobs for the same reason.) So my mother threw her considerable, extravagant energy into shopping and playing cards. Later, after we'd moved to the suburbs, she added golf and volunteering for Hadassah, of which she was president for years.

My mother played canasta, bridge, and mah-jongg. My father played pinochle with his friends. I was fascinated with the mah-jongg tiles, the click they made as they were played, and the long leather box they came in. I was fascinated by the talk around the pinochle table, the cigar smoke, the scorekeeping, and the exchange of money at the end. I never learned any of these games. Even now I have a distaste for most games. When I compare them to an evening of watching television, though, they seem preferable, having at least an element of human contact.

Looking back, I saw my mother's life as empty. It wasn't, of course. It was full of activities that her restlessness and fast metabolism required to keep her from going crazy with boredom. But it was empty of that soft and nurturing affection that I think of now as mothering. My mother's children were pawns in a game of cobbling together a sense of self-worth. I think my brother passed the test, but I never did. I was too skinny, mean to her, too quiet, shy, not pretty and not popular, smart but not dazzling—not a prize-winner. I was lazy, slow, had no friends, stayed indoors too much, read too much, and did something for which she had no category and no tolerance—I sat and thought.

"What are you doing?" she would ask, meaning I should be doing something else.

"Thinking," I would say.
"You mean you're just sitting there thinking?"
"Yes."
"Why?"
"Don't you ever just sit and think?"
"No."
Of course, I knew that, but what else was there to say?

EARLIEST MEMORIES

I AM IN THE CRIB, *needing something but not crying because I don't want my mother to show up. I am afraid of her. This is not a memory but an intuitive record that comes unbidden when I try to remember.*

As a baby: neglected and despised, fearful, timid, paralyzed, but at the same time with a secret core of joy. All through my unhappy childhood I knew joy existed, just beyond the edges of my life, and I hated to hear the fairy tales that created complications and frustrations for their heroes—I wanted all stories to go smoothly and have a happy ending.

I wake in the middle of the night needing to pee, and stand up in my crib, intending to ask to be taken to the bathroom. I look over at the bed where Kate, the maid, sleeps and see someone sleeping there. It's Thursday, Kate's night out. I say uh-oh, thinking it's a stranger. I'm afraid of the stranger, and decide to lie down again and pee in my bed. In the morning I get into trouble for wetting my bed. When I explain to Kate that there was a stranger in her bed she laughs at me and says, "That was me! I came home in the middle of the night."

A darker memory from before that: Somehow, I have been left alone in our apartment. I must be around two, because we moved from this place before my brother was born, when I was three and a half. I wander into the dark hall looking for my mother and I knock over the telephone, which sits on a little table. I am frightened of the noise, frightened of the dark, and I don't know where my mother is. I'm crying. At that moment she comes back, laughing as she walks in the front door. All my adult life I've been afraid of the telephone. I jump when it rings. I put off phone calls for as long as I can, sometimes for years. I avoid making calls whenever possible, even though there are costs involved. It never occurred to me to connect this with that early experience, until suddenly, one day, it did.

My aunt and uncle lived in the same building. One day I am sent on a big-girl errand to go upstairs and tell my aunt something. I go up the stairs, getting farther and farther from familiar territory. I arrive at the door I remember as theirs, and I ring the bell. As I wait in the dark hall for someone to come I become convinced that I have rung the wrong doorbell, and I turn around and run away. I get back to our apartment and tell my mother I couldn't find the right door. She is annoyed.

I am two. My father, who spends half the week on the road selling his costume jewelry to department stores, sends me a letter. On it he has drawn Felix the Cat. I am delighted with the drawing, which is black, and bigger than anything else in the letter. Years later I find that letter in my mother's drawer. He says in it that he can't wait to get home to hug me and kiss me. My father has beautiful handwriting.

Again, I am maybe two. My parents and I are going for a stroll on the path that circles the aqueduct near our house. It is winter, I guess, because my mother is wearing a black sealskin coat, as soft as a cloud. I hold her hand for a while and then walk on alone, spaced out in some other world where little kids can go and the rest of us can't. At one point I find myself again walking next to the soft black fur coat, and I reach up and take the hand beside me. A strange face looks down at me. I am shaken to the core. Where is my mother? Who is this? I hear laughter behind me, and turn to see my mother and father and their friends laughing at me. I am devastated and humiliated.

At the age of two and a half I am sent to camp for two weeks. I remember my mother saying she had to talk them into taking me because I was so young. I also remember sitting on a bed surrounded by other kids, all older than I am. They seem huge to me. They were probably six. I think they were making a fuss over me because I'm just a baby. I am utterly bewildered in this scene. I don't know what the fuss is about.

I am two or three. I am sitting on the beach in Far Rockaway, at the edge of the water, my toes in the little lapping wavelets. Next to me is Billy, the son of my parents' closest friends, and my best friend. He is a year older than me. Far out to sea, on the horizon, is a large ship—maybe an ocean liner. I am crying in fear because I'm sure the ship is coming straight at me and is going to run over me. Billy is saying, reasonably, "It's far away. It can't get here," but I am not reassured. My mother calls my name and I turn around. She has put her bathing cap on top of her head and is making funny faces at me, trying to get me to stop crying. I am not comforted.

*I am almost three. I am playing in the courtyard of our apartment building with a group of friends. One of my friends calls me "Dragon Lady" because she says I have slanted eyes. (Dragon Lady was a character from one of our beloved comic books—*Terry and the Pirates.*) In a ground floor apartment lives a girl much older than I am, probably six years old. She sits at the open window and talks to us. She is disabled, and spends her life in a wheelchair, often sitting at the window. She specializes in making beaded objects on a small loom. She offers to make me a beaded bracelet with my name on it. I of course accept. The next day she gives it to me, a band of beads that goes around my wrist and says ELLIN in blue beads. I am proud of it.*

I am three and a half—my brother would be born later that year, in October. I have been sent to the beach—Far Rockaway—with my grandfather and cousins. There are at least eight cousins, all older than I. It's hard for me now to picture all those little kids under the care of my grandfather, who was for me a remote and intimidating figure. I remember little of that day, except for the thing that happened to me.

We go into the water to play Ring Around the Rosie. The water isn't deep—deeper for me than for the others, but surely not higher than my waist. We hold hands and start to sing, going round in a circle as we sing. I remember being confused, not knowing what I am supposed to do. I remember going under the water and seeing the legs of my cousins, still in a ring. Everyone gets up except me. They keep going round. Nobody notices I am gone. Then a woman on shore notices, and shouts. I don't remember this part. The next thing I remember is coming awake lying over a barrel. I vaguely remember vomiting. There is a crowd around me.

The way I remember being over a barrel is looking at myself from behind, a short distance away. I am holding the hand of someone taller than I. I think I am being delivered back to my body in that scene.

I don't remember anyone ever talking to me about what happened, though I do remember my mother talking about it to others. I remember her saying that the only one who noticed that I wasn't there was a woman on the beach. Do I remember a slight tone of enjoyment, at having a good story to tell? I think I also remember her annoyance at my grandfather—he hadn't done a good job.

I read once that people who have near-death experiences can't keep watches going. I read it with astonishment, because my watches broke continually all my life. I could wear a watch for about three months, and then it would mysteriously stop working. I could get it fixed, but it was never the same. Even my clocks keep bizarre time, though I seem to have got the fluctuations down to plus or minus five minutes, which is usable. My solution has been to buy cheap watches, and when they break, throw them away.

I am four. I am sent to nursery school. I learn a few words of French there: brun, rouge, bleu. *We are also taught to dance, ballroom dancing. I dance with a boy named Noel. He has a sweet round face and smooth blond hair, and he is gentle and mild for a boy. We talk as we dance. I am thinking, "We are just like grownups, dancing and talking."*

I am four or five. We have gone for a walk on the Grand Concourse (in the Bronx.) My mother and father are there. My mother is pushing my brother in the baby carriage. There's another family with us—either my aunt and uncle and their children, or my parents' closest friends, Sibby and Paul, whom I call aunt and uncle, and their son Billy, still my best friend. The grown-ups stop

~14~

at a stand selling soft ice cream and I am offered an ice cream cone, my first. It is piled high with a pyramid of pale chocolate ice cream. I take a few licks and throw up on the street. There is a loud commotion around me. After that, I refuse to eat ice cream. I don't start to really like it until I am in my sixties. Even in Paris, where they have Berthillon, which is arguably the best ice cream in the world, I don't eat it. My daughter and her friends line up in the block-long queue on the Ile Saint-Louis to wait their turn to order a cone, but not me. When I walk around the Ile I often see the line of thirty or so people waiting for Berthillon ice cream, but I walk by, not tempted. Some events have long legs. I got over it, though. Now when I am in Paris in the summer I head straight for Berthillon and manage to have to pass it at least once a day.

ᑫ TWO

The Bronx

I SUPPOSE THERE WAS A TIME when people who lived to be seventy found themselves in the same world they'd lived in when they were young, only they'd grown older. Not now. My contemporaries and I have lived through a time when the accelerating rate of change has sped us along to inhabit a different world from the one we grew up in.

The Bronx of my early years was a quiet and leisurely place, almost pastoral compared to now. There were few cars. We lived on Buchanan Place, a street of five-story brick buildings sprinkled with two-story private houses. There was a grocery store across the street and a candy store with a little window that opened to the street, and through which the owner could pass newspapers to grownups and candy to the kids. Inside was a long glass case full of penny candies: shoe leather, yellow spongy peanut-shaped marshmallows, bubble gum chunks wrapped in comics, little chocolate disks sprinkled with white dots, brown chocolate babies, Tootsie Roll lollipops, little hearts with messages stamped on them—some of those candies are still around. A penny in your fist let you spend an exciting ten minutes gazing at the delicious treasures before choosing one. My little brother and I went together, and he tells me I was too shy to ask for my candy, so he had to do it for me.

I accompanied my mother on her shopping trips to the neighborhood stores that supplied our food. I liked going to the dairy, where she bought butter that was cut with a knife from large wooden tubs brought down from a high (to me) shelf—"Salt or sweet?" An irregular two-pound chunk wrapped in thick white paper went into her shopping bag. We didn't buy milk there—the milk was delivered every morning in glass bottles by the friendly milkman dressed in a white uniform who stopped to chat briefly and ask if we wanted cottage cheese today. We took our laundry to the Chinese man whose steamy shop was across the street from our apartment house. He gave me dried lichee nuts, which I regarded with suspicion but ate because my mother didn't urge me to. The errand I dreaded was the butcher shop with its cheery men in blood-stained white aprons behind the counter wielding cleavers and cutting bloody red meat into family-sized pieces. I hung back, not wanting to go in, while my mother pulled me by the arm impatiently. "Don't be such a sissy." Many years later when I became a vegetarian I remembered this scene and felt in it a premonition of my choosing not to eat meat.

The street was colorful. I loved the horse-drawn wagon that delivered ice, not to us because we had an electric refrigerator with a large white coil on the top, but to others in our building. The iceman carried it up the stairs on his back and heaved the blocks around with his giant tongs. From time to time a man came by with a pushcart and sang out "I—cash—clothes." Women brought their old clothes out to him and he looked through them and bought some. My mother and I watched from our fourth-floor window. Once in a while a street musician came by, singing songs loudly as he looked up at the windows of our building. My mother and other women whose windows faced the street would wrap coins in pieces of white paper and toss them down to the singer, who gathered them from the sidewalk, waving thanks.

In the world of my childhood when you made a phone call you called the operator on a telephone shaped like a black daffodil. "Number please?" she asked, and you told her the number you wanted, and she connected you. The phone numbers were preceded by place names: Murray Hill, Rhinelander, and then four numbers. The name of your exchange mattered. Some were better than others.

Since there were not many cars in the Bronx in those days, it was a major event when my father and his oldest friend bought a car together for the two families to share. They parked it downstairs on the side street below my bedroom window, where it was an object of pride and reverence. My parents took rides in it around the aqueduct nearby, and my father and his friend drove it on Sunday mornings to go play tennis. Once I was offered the treat of going for a ride after dinner, if I took a nap. I lay down on my bed and fell asleep and woke up the next morning, full of woe. My mother told me they didn't want to wake me. The disappointment still stings.

On weekends our family went for a promenade along a path by the aqueduct, two blocks from our building—one of the attractions of the place where we lived. Many families made this promenade—a New York paseo. On Saturdays my mother took me to a movie and left me there—a magical baby sitter. Saturday afternoon at the movies. Small-town stuff.

CR

Sometime before my brother was born, in my third year, we moved to a new apartment. It was lighter and had two bedrooms and a big living room that was two steps down from the foyer (considered a desirable feature in those days, though I can't imagine why). In the living room we had a baby grand piano and a plant with tall blade-like leaves with a green-yellow border around them. The kitchen had a table where we ate, and from the kitchen window we could see the corner grocery store across the street. When we visited the apartment before moving in my father joked that he could call out the window and ask them to send up groceries. I believed he was really going to do that, and I thought it was a good idea.

Our two-bedroom apartment cost $25 a month, and so did our full-time, live-in maid. Or rather our series of maids, mostly young Polish Catholic country girls, who came to New York from Pennsylvania looking for jobs. My favorite was Kate, probably because she stayed long enough to become part of my family in memory. Kate was from Johnstown, and she filled my quivering mind with horror stories—about the Johnstown flood, ghosts her father had seen, and, worst of all, "The Monkey's Paw," the W.W. Jacobs short story about a man who wishes for the return of his dead son and just as he hears a knocking at the door, changes his mind. This story hid in a dark corner of my memory and terrified me until I was about college age. Kate took me to see movies, and made fun of me when I cried at *The Biscuit Eater* ("You don't cry for people, but you cry for a dog!"). I was fond of Kate, and I missed her when she left. Love was scarce in my life.

The front door of our apartment was opposite the kitchen door, and around the corner was a hall in front of the two bedrooms, where I spent a lot of my time. There was a full-length mirror in the hallway. Years later, in psychoanalysis, I would look into this mirror in my memory and see no one reflected. My bedroom and my parents' bedroom were side by side and looked out on the side street. I was given a bed in my new bedroom. The crib would be my brother's. Kate also slept there. In my parents' bedroom the bed was against a corner of the room at an angle, and that's another place where I spent a lot of time—between the headboard and the corner walls, in a little triangular-shaped hideaway.

The school I went to was two blocks from our house, and I walked there alone every day. In those days the streets were innocent, and there was no need to protect kids from what might happen there. The worst thing that happened to me was meeting a girl, the friend of a friend, on the way to kindergarten one day, and getting into a heated argument with her. I asked her name, and she said "Ellen."

"No, it's not," I said indignantly, "*I'm* Ellin."

"No, I am," she insisted, and we fought about it all the way to school.

We kids had the run of the street. We stayed on the sidewalk, of course, or played in the vacant lot two doors down. The lot was scrubby, but it was a taste of nature. There were weeds and trees and a few bushes to hide behind. Every evening we were out there playing together after dinner—until 7:30, that is, when I had a sacred date with *The Lone Ranger*. My parents would call my name from the kitchen window and I would go running upstairs to listen to the radio for half an hour.

Books were my other escape. I read hungrily—*Grimm's Fairy Tales*, *Andersen's Fairy Tales*, *Pinocchio*, and *A Child's Garden of Verses*. All those books, which I still have, are covered with my drawings on the end pages, and sometimes even in the text. I drew girls with long hair, standing or lying down, and sometimes with a column of tears falling from each eye to the ground in neat rows. In one drawing there are little buckets to catch the tears. I used every scrap of empty paper I could get my hands on to do my drawings. They are all over my books and on the backs of envelopes. Although my uncle was a paper manufacturer and had a closet full of pads that made me shiver in wonder when I saw it, nobody seems to have thought to give me a drawing pad. Money was tight in those days, and paper for kids to draw on must have seemed like an unthinkable luxury.

One night, years later when I was a young mother, I put my kids to bed and sat down in the living room to read. I had just come across my old and worn copy of *Grimm's Fairy Tales*, which I hadn't read since childhood. I opened the book to the first story, "The Frog Prince." As I read the first few lines I found myself propelled in an instant into a world I had not been in since early childhood. The princess, the frog, the golden ball, and the pond were all real and present—as real as the room I sat in, more real, maybe, though the reality was internal. There are not adequate words to describe the state I was in. There was no reality beyond the magical one my mind had created, and I was fully present there. As it is in a dream, I was unaware of the room around me. I stayed there for long minutes and then gradually, reluctantly, came back to my adult mind. I was overwhelmed with awe at the glimpse I'd been given of that utterly otherworldly world I had once inhabited.

Movies transported us too. We acted out movies we'd seen. (I still remember *Wagon Train*.) We talked about airplanes—German ones and American ones. America wasn't in the war yet, but its shadow fell across our play. We talked about baseball players—there were only the Dodgers and the Yankees, and you were one or the other. The Giants existed at the fuzzy edge of this world, and there was absolutely no one else. I was a Yankee. I knew nothing about baseball, except that you played it with a bat.

I remember I had a woolen snowsuit with a pointed hat,

like a witch's hat or a dunce cap—it was gray with red trim and tied under my chin. I wore it when I played outside in the snow in front of our apartment building with a group of kids who lived on our block. We would build snow forts. One time, when I had climbed up the side of the fort and slid down, I fell on my back and got the wind knocked out of me. It felt radical. I couldn't breathe. I thrashed around and tried to draw a breath, and the other kids watched me and laughed. Eventually I could breathe again. It was frightening.

Our toys were primitive. I remember using little broken twigs as cereal in my play bowl, and my toy animals were lengths of chain my father brought home from his costume jewelry business. I turned them into snakes of different colors and played with them for hours. I had one spectacular doll, given to me by one of my aunts. She was a Princess Elizabeth doll with pink porcelain cheeks and blue-green eyes that opened and closed. In her gold-blond curls sat a diamond tiara, and her dress was long and pleated and pink and silk. She was almost two feet long, and I played with her very carefully. I still have her. Her head has come loose, her golden curls are bedraggled, her dress has holes and her tiara is broken and flops down in the middle. She has grown old along with me.

I had two boyfriends while we lived in that apartment. One, Monte, lived in our building, upstairs on the fifth floor. We were friends, and everyone said he was my boyfriend. He was a grade ahead of me at school. Many years later he found me again when we were both at college, and he invited me to visit him one weekend. I went and had a great time with him. I liked him very much. Whatever happened to Monte?

My other boyfriend was Eliot, a wild kid from across the street. His mother was a hairdresser and his father didn't live with them, a very rare thing in those days. Eliot was a little bit dangerous, not quite like us, but he really loved me. One night he rang the bell of our apartment and when my mother opened the door he threw a little package of wadded paper in and ran away. Inside were a green glass ring and a note: "Please do me a fafer and be my girlfriend." Eliot took me occasionally to one of his favorite hangouts, a store under the El (the elevated subway train several blocks from my apartment) where you could buy old, beat-up comic books for a penny, instead of the ten cents you had to pay for a new one. They were in piles on the floor, thousands of them. I loved comic books—we all did. We read *Superman* and *Wonder Woman* and *Archie,* and traded them with each other. If I still had them they'd probably be worth a fortune now. (I have my Princess Elizabeth doll, but she is not in mint condition.)

When the baby grand moved with us to the suburbs, some years later, I took piano lessons on it, desultory affairs in which I displayed neither talent nor appetite for learning the piano. I much preferred my grandmother's player piano, which played whole songs without requiring anyone's labor, the black and white keys pumping up and down magically like ghost tracks, and tinny songs noodling out as the hole-punched paper scrolled around a cylinder.

My grandmother had another object I envied: a tall and bulky wooden Victrola on which she played old wax records, including one of Caruso scratchily singing "O Sole Mio." To hear the greatness of a voice you have to hear it in person, or else on the technical wizardry of a modern sound system.

I also remember a little table in our apartment that was mine. It was enameled a pale green and had the alphabet enameled on it in darker green, starting on the left side and going up to G, where it turned a corner and marched straight over to U and then went down the right side to Z. The alphabet still has that shape to me. Up, over, and down. G is in the left corner and U is in the right.

The objects I remember are so different from the ones we have now. Today, my camera slips into my pocket. My parents had a Kodak camera that was a long thin black box, which opened to reveal a lens and a black bellows that accordion-folded out, and back into the box when it was closed. My parents were proud of it, and kept it in a dresser drawer in their bedroom. (They were devastated when the camera was stolen on a trip to Mexico.) My mother's baby grand piano would fill up half my living room, even though I live in relative luxury. My grandchildren have a roomful of toys ten times bigger than the ones my grandmother brought in her cardboard box, and much more numerous. My clothes are sewn on a machine in China or the Philippines, and no one cares if the seams are sewn straight.

CR

My brother was born when I was three and a half. I remember the day they brought him home. A big, fat, friendly black nurse, Miss Mitchell, came along to take care of him for a while. What I remember is lying on my bed as the three of them—my mother, my father, and Miss Mitchell—changed his diaper in the bathroom, suddenly screaming with laughter because he had peed high into the air. Even though I was only three and a half, I knew that meant something: my life was changing.

The myth in our family was that my mother didn't want to have children yet but my father wanted one—me. The second time, my father didn't want to have two, but my mother wanted another—my brother. Thus I became my father's little girl, and my brother belonged to my mother.

My brother was famous. He was the terror of the neighborhood. The ladies who sat outside our building on the sidewalk talking and rocking their baby carriages got up and left when they saw him coming. And no wonder—he was fond of throwing rocks straight up in the air and letting them come down where they would. He also liked riding down the hill next to our house on his tricycle with his legs on the handlebars and his head flung behind, hanging over the seat. My mother complained, but with a touch of pride in her voice, bragging.

I felt displaced by my brother's arrival. My loneliness increased by the amount of attention that he commanded, partly because he was a boy and partly because he was such a high-energy kid. Not that I had felt secure before—I was timid and afraid and was always being yelled at for sins I didn't understand. But once my brother came he became a focus of attention in a way I had never been, and I knew myself to be not only unimportant, but of lesser importance. The full force of the difference became clear to me in a flash of insight one day when I came home from kindergarten and, walking in the door, saw my mother and my brother sitting together on the floor at the far end of the living room, laughing. She was playing with him. I realized in that moment that he and I had different mothers.

I was an artist by the time I was two and a half. I have seen drawings I did at that age, wonderfully complex line drawings of a fisherman, a hippopotamus, and a circus on wheels. I don't know if I would have blossomed and expanded if I had been encouraged. Instead I drew on scraps of paper or in coloring books, where I was told to color inside the lines, and my drawings were criticized for what they were not. I became timid and lacking in self-confidence, not just in art but in who I was.

Although low on the totem pole at home, I shone at school, in a muted way. The acknowledgements were often indirect, but I got the idea, reinforcing my family's image of me, that I was smart. In second grade our class went on a trip to the zoo, and that night for homework I wrote a poem about it. The teacher didn't believe I'd written the poem myself, and required me to sit down at my desk and write another poem then and there, which I did. Nobody said, "Wow, good poem!" but my zoo poem went into the school newspaper.

I was timid and shy to the point of pathology, afraid to ask for my candy at the candy store, afraid to ask my mother to lend me her pretty hat for the school play. I was the girl from Paris in the third-grade play, and my line was, "I bring the latest styles from Paris." My teacher asked me if my mother had a pretty hat I could borrow for the play. I said I would ask her, but I never did. I told my teacher she had said, "No." The teacher said, "That's okay, I'll lend you mine." So I went out on the stage and held up the dowdy brown hat she wore to school every day and said my line about the latest styles from Paris, and the audience burst into laughter. At that moment I realized what a bad scene it was—how it must have hurt my teacher, how awful it was that I couldn't ask my mother for her hat, and how horrible it was to stand there with everyone laughing at me.

While my memory is of being timid, scared, isolated, and miserable as a child, years later, in psychoanalysis, I suddenly recalled that I was elected president of my first-grade class. I always got excellent grades in school, but I never won any honors. I had boyfriends, admirers. But other children made fun of me. Within myself—maybe by nature—I was joyful, creative, competent, intelligent, but I saw myself and was seen in my family as a failure, not good enough, scorned. It was the beginning of not having a clue to who I was, a state that lasted into my thirties. My life stayed on this track through grammar school and high school. I never managed to rescue myself from this fog of unknowing. It was only when I was accepted to Wellesley and went off to college that I was able to try out life on my own.

I never really got over my timidity—I just got bigger. When I was in fourth grade, we moved to a new house in Mount Vernon, the suburbs. My classmates at my new school saw me as the new kid on the block, and offered their interest. But I couldn't behave like the others, and did things that alienated me from them, soon creating for myself the role of outcast—the only role I inhabited comfortably for most of my young years. By comfortable I mean the same word that applies to an old and worn piece of clothing. It's faded and torn and ugly, and you look messy in it, but it has become like a second skin, and in it you feel like you.

When I went away to college, I kept that outfit, but I got a new one too. I was with girls of high intelligence and achievement and, in the bargain, high social class, and while I was incapable of making many friends, I did get a new outfit I could put on at will—the veneer of social and intellectual competence. Eventually, I became able to wear that outfit more often than not, and my outcast nature became a lot less visible. The mere fact that I had been accepted at Wellesley, and that these girls were my peers, gave me a small measure of self-confidence that smoothed over some of the rough edges of my ragged soul.

◊

My mother lived in constant anxiety about me. She was convinced I didn't measure up. Her sisters, large and imposing women with loud, confident voices, were all older than my mother. Their children were plump, as children should be. I was skinny. Eating was a constant battle between us, and I eventually got really good at not eating anything, and especially not drinking my milk. I would sit endlessly over a glass of milk, not allowed to leave the table until I finished it, which was going to be never. After a while the maid or my mother would get tired of watching me and leave, and I would pour the milk down the sink. Didn't anyone ever catch on?

There is a photograph of me in existence somewhere, lost for the moment but lodged safely in my memory, in which I am standing alone smiling. I'm wearing a dress with a sailor collar. The photo is black and white, or rather shades of gray, but I remember the dress well. It was yellow with white stripes around the collar and sleeves and a little brown anchor in each corner of the wide sailor collar. My hair is blond, cut short to just below my ears and pulled to one side in a barrette. My smiling cheeks are pudgy with baby fat, so I am three or four. I am standing on the little second-floor porch of my Aunt Sue's house; the brick wall of the porch is the backdrop behind me. My smile is fake. It is a well-remembered smile, the one I grew all on my own to hide my feelings. Maybe to someone else it looks like a family-album picture of a child, but to me it is a picture of loneliness. One leg is crossed over the other because I had to pee, something I would never tell anyone. How did I learn to hide so thoroughly at such a tender age? Only necessity could have taught me so well.

I see in my mind's eye a cute little girl. It took me many years to see it that way. The epithet for me in my family was, "She's not pretty, but boy is she smart." They actually told me that. My mother repeated it to me often. Such simple words, but they defined my life in so many ways. When I felt I was nothing else of any worth, I always felt I was smart. And not until I was well into my fifties did it truly come to me that I am not ugly. Looking back, I see that I expended huge amounts of energy in my life trying to be something I already was. Hiding became a way of life, which age has freed me from. There was not enough love for the little girl in the photo, but now I love her.

Looking now at the few baby pictures of me, I have no idea why it was that I was seen as "not pretty," which implies a striking degree of not pretty that I can't find in those pictures. But true or not, it marked me, as did "boy, is she smart." My mother used to sing to me—one of the few memories of tenderness I have of her. When she sang the lullaby that ended "while my little one, while my pretty one sleeps," I used to think sleepily, "I'm the little one, but who's the pretty one?" That was before my brother was born. He turned out to be the pretty one.

One day I witnessed my mother sitting next to the baby grand piano being flirty and giggly with the man who had come to pick up the laundry. He had pulled out his scale—a long flat brass stick with a large solid hook on the end and weights marked along its length, with which he weighed our laundry, which was wrapped up in a sheet like a hobo's bundle or the sack a boy puts on the end of stick and rests on his shoulder when he runs away from home. The laundry man says something and laughs, and my mother laughs. I am shocked and a little frightened. I must have been around four. I had no concept of flirty behavior, but the scene is stored in my memory banks with that label. The whole scene is picture-clear to me now, and as I look at it again I see that I am frightened because my mother is laughing. Have I not seen her laugh before? Am I just becoming aware that she is different for others than she is for me? Many years later I bought a scale like that in the Paris flea market. I still have it.

In another memory, I am lying in bed, sick, feverish, and my mother is standing over me. Once again, she is laughing, but at me. Why? Why are you laughing at me, Mother? What a strange scene.

I remember thinking when I was very young that there were things I would know after I was dead, but not until then. And when my feelings were crushed, for comfort, I would tell myself, "This won't matter after I'm dead." Now I find that a strange thought for a four-year-old, but then it was just one of my thoughts. I also thought that the gloom I lived in was just life—that everyone's life was like that. The gloom I lived in was the creation of my mother's venomous attacks on me, along with her total lack of loving support. I'm sure she thought she was just trying to improve me, since I fell so short of perfection. To me it was simply a world in which I was not good enough, would never be good enough, could never be good enough, not just for her, but for anyone.

I got my first conscious inkling of something different when I was around five and went with a friend to her apartment. We went into the kitchen where her mother stood at the stove wearing an apron. Her mother heard us and turned with a smile to greet her little girl. She and my friend talked to each other, smiled and laughed. A new possibility entered my consciousness and stayed there vividly enough so that I can still see it in my mind's eye close to seventy years later. I am standing at the door of the kitchen. My friend's mother is across the room at the stove. I am looking up at her back. I see her apron, with flowers on it. It's the kind you put on over your head—it has a front and a back. She is ample and has reddish-brown frizzy hair. I hardly see my friend at her side. I don't remember her name. I was utterly astonished that a mother could talk to a daughter like that. It was a new concept to me—a loving mother—but it did not translate into my mind or seem to apply to me. In other words, I didn't think, "I wish I had a mother like that." It was like seeing some bizarre and wonderful animal at the zoo.

I think about who I might have been with different parents, but what does it matter? I would have been someone else. I have made my way from there to who I am now, and the journey is part of my existence. The fact that it was hard gives it depth and shapes my consciousness. Our journeys are all hard, in one way or another. I was wounded in something that was central to my life—my art—and in my ability to love and feel loved. To the extent that I have recovered from those wounds through my own effort, I am a hero, as are we all.

☙

Here is the poem I wrote on command in second grade. It's based on the musical piece "Danse Macabre," which our teacher explained to us and then played for us that morning.

Danse Macabre

The night was dark and all was still
When a cry rang out—it was clear and shrill.
It came from a graveyard dark and damp
Where Death stood, holding a lighted lamp.

He took a fiddle from under a stone,
The bow was made of a skeleton's bone.
He struck up a tune with a magic sound
And the skeletons came from out of the ground.

They danced and spread the gossip around
Until they heard their parting sound.
A rooster had crowed, loud and shrill.
They went back to their graves and again all was still.

GIFTS

MY PARENTS' PENDULUM SWUNG FROM *being stingy and withhold-ing to being lavish with material gifts. The withholding part trained me not to risk wanting things, so when the lavish gifts came they were mostly unwanted.*

I remember as a little girl spending some weeks of the summer at the country hotel owned by my father's brothers. The hotel had a small candy store and my cousins and I were sometimes given money to buy ourselves a piece of candy. I remember going crying to my mother because the candy cost a nickel, which my cousins all had, but I had been given a penny and couldn't buy any candy. I don't remember whether I was then given a nickel—somehow I don't think so—but the charge of the disappointment stayed fresh, and must carry with it a weight of other experiences for which it stands.

When I went to summer camp at the age of fourteen I was with a group of girls who already had a certain amount of social experi-ence, unlike me. We had weekend dances with the boys' camp every Saturday night, and the uniform was the same for all the girls: a sweater and slacks. The girls in my bunk had cubbies piled high with sweaters of different colors—two rows of neatly folded sweaters, four or five in each row. In those days a sweater was either a pull-over with a round neck or a cardigan with little mother-of-pearl buttons, which we wore buttoned in the back. All that distinguished the sweaters from each other was their color. Sweaters of different shapes and thicknesses, sweaters with designs knit into them, all ap-peared much later, years later. So the cubbies were piled with row on row of colors—pink, blue, green, yellow, white, black—but my cub-by had only two sweaters. I felt humiliated, inferior, but we never talked about it. I don't think my parents were poorer than the other girls' families, I think they just weren't used to providing clothes for me in those quantities.

When I was thirteen my father went away on a business trip and came home with presents for the whole family. Mine was a red umbrella with a snakeskin sleeve. It was so elegant and sophisticated, it was way beyond my ability to relate to it, much less desire it. Still, I recognized how special it was and felt enormous pride that it was mine. My mother also recognized how special it was, and announced that it was way too adult and expensive a gift for me, and my father must have meant it for her. So she took it, and it became hers. The first time she carried it she left the snakeskin sleeve in a taxi.

Remembering the feelings of that experience reminds me of one that preceded it by years. One Easter my parents had guests for the evening. We never acknowledged the existence of Easter in my home. Christmas was bad enough—a glittering holiday for almost everyone, which we, being Jewish, did not get to share. Easter, with the Easter bunny and Easter eggs and palms and ashes, was simply exotic and foreign, like an Indian rain dance. We were way, way on the outside, not even looking in. But my parents' guests brought me a chocolate Easter bunny—my first, and the only one I ever had. It was awesome, about seven inches high, and all chocolate, and though it was hollow, I saw at once that it was a lot of chocolate. It stood on its hind legs, its paws held up at its chest, and it had a red ribbon around its neck. It was my treasure. My mother told me to put it in the refrigerator, since I was on my way to bed, and I could have some tomorrow morning. When I woke up the next morning I ran downstairs to claim it from the refrigerator. It was half gone. My mother had eaten the top half of the bunny. She told me it was too much chocolate for me. The sense of betrayal was beyond words, was like a cold climate in my inner being. I felt helpless, and utterly without recourse. I think that experience somehow prepared the ground for the taking of the umbrella—in some perverse way, it softened the blow of the new betrayal, which was now more or less what I had come to expect.

I asked my parents persistently for a dog. They would always

answer the same thing. "Can I have a dog?" "Yes, when you're good."
They knew, and I came to learn, when that was going to be. It gave
me (one of their gifts) the pervasive, undoubted, and hopeless con-
viction that not only was I not good and would never be good, but
there was not even any hope, any possibility, of being good. Sometime
around my thirteenth year my mother's sister offered her her own
dog, a fox terrier. The dog came home as my mother's dog. Within a
week of the dog's arrival I went into the kitchen, where my mother
sat, with a rose petal pressed between my lips, saying, "Look—I have
rosy lips!" The dog took one look, leaped up at me and bit me in the
stomach. That was the end of dogs in our house. I had already by that
time adapted by having an imaginary dog, a big shaggy collie, tall as
my waist, who walked me to school and loved me.

For my thirteenth birthday my aunt—my mother's sister-in-
law and an outsider in the family because she was considered aloof—
gave me a memorable present. She gave me a box of watercolors,
with a wheel of colors inside that surpassed my imagination for
what color could be. Not simply blue and yellow and red and green,
but blue-green and blue-violet and yellow-green and red-orange,
and more. I loved that box so much I couldn't bring myself to use it. I
still have it now, in my early seventies. And that outsider aunt, un-
appreciated by her in-law family, has my undying gratitude. When
I married she gave me a featherweight Singer sewing machine—
another one of my all-time great presents.

Aunt Essie.

Toward the end of World War II my cousin was sent to Burma.
Because my father designed and made jewelry, my cousin wrote to
him asking whether he could use inexpensive star sapphires, which
were plentiful there. My father wrote back and asked him to send
a sample. He sent a small star sapphire, dome-shaped and very
flawed, with a dimple of rough-looking rock on the side of it. My
father wrote back and said he couldn't use them, and then surprised
me with a ring he designed and had made for me. The sapphire was
in the center, surrounded by ten pink rubies and set in pink gold. It

was a charming ring, perfect for a young girl, and I loved it, and still love it. It's a bond between my father and me.

When I graduated from high school my father gave me a gold watch with a gold watchband. It was beautiful and I was thrilled and impressed. It had a serious flaw, though—the buckle slid open and the watch fell off. It was the first of the problematic gifts of gold watches my parents gave me. My mother got into the habit of giving me expensive watches that she had once coveted but was now tired of and wanted to replace. She gave me a pink-gold watch with rubies set around the face. I couldn't wear it—I couldn't even relate to it. I stuck it in my drawer, and one day it disappeared. Another time she gave me a mink stole. A mink stole! My son Jonathan, who was about two, called it my Davy Crockett.

During psychoanalysis I had a dream that my parents were throwing gold watches at me.

The gifts my parents gave me were well-meaning attempts to make me happy with the things that would have made them happy. The effort was doomed, though, because they had already trained me to feel that wanting things was dangerous, and left me vulnerable to being manipulated and controlled. I am not able to figure out whether my lack of desire for material luxuries is my nature, or whether it's the result of early childhood experiences. In a way I look at the deprivations of my childhood as a blessing, because they sent me in the direction of simplicity that I appreciate more and more as I move more firmly and consciously into it.

♋ THREE

The War

W HEN RUMBLINGS OF WAR STARTED in the 1930s I was a kid—six or seven or eight. We began to hear stories of Jews leaving Germany, and at one point my parents received a letter from some Czechoslovakian Jews with a name similar to our name, Randel. They were trying to find out if we were related, and if we could help them get out of Czechoslovakia. My parents talked about the letter in front of me, and clearly took it seriously. I don't know what they did about it.

When war was declared, there was a sense of high drama that I didn't understand but did feel. There were changes in our lives, but to me they were minor. We were issued rationing coupons, which meant that we had to be careful about the use of butter or sugar or meat, and sometimes people swapped coupons to take care of special needs. Gas was rationed, so trips had to be planned and allowed for. We didn't use our car a lot, so it didn't have much impact on me. We still went to visit my relatives in New Jersey, but it was a trip that was carefully calculated.

My parents seemed to take the war in stride. At the beginning it made little change in our lives. I remember asking them if we weren't supposed to wash out our tin cans and flatten them and turn them in. My mother told me we didn't have to do that. It left me with the unfortunate impression that the rules didn't apply to us. Later we did do it. I don't know what changed. I read only recently that it was mostly a symbolic exercise, intended to give people the feeling of participating actively in what was called "the war effort."

I had two cousins who went to war, and a fifth-grade home-room teacher, Mr. Lewis. He bid us a contained but emotional goodbye, and left in the middle of the term. It was unnerving, but we were on the whole unaware of the full implications of his leaving. He was one of those who didn't come back. A counselor from the camp I went to also left and didn't come back. My two cousins went to exotic places—Marvin to Burma and Murray to the Philippines. They both came back at the end of the war—one of them with malaria, which recurred in attacks throughout the rest of his life.

My father became an air-raid warden, which meant that when there was an air-raid alert, he put on the yellow hard hat that had been issued to him and went out to patrol the neighborhood, making sure our suburban neighbors didn't have any lights showing. We were required to either turn out all the house lights for the duration of the alert, or to block them totally with dark curtains at the windows that didn't allow even a sliver of light to show through. The streetlights went out also. I believe my father had a special air-raid warden flashlight so he could see his way around the block in the dark. The alerts were usually brief, and the all-clear would sound after ten minutes or so and allow everyone to go back to normal. There were never any planes overhead, and as we all know, we never got bombed. It's hard not to absorb a sense of being privileged when you know that places in the world are going through chaos, and you are only being asked to do without some butter and some trips in the car.

We kids, along with everyone else, were taught to hate the Germans and the "Japs." We were supposed to hate the Italians too, but the propaganda was less intense and I don't remember wasting much energy on hating Italians. We hated bad Germans and made fun of the Fuehrer and sang hate songs about the war and songs about, "I'll be faithful till you come home," a concept that went over my head at the time. It never occurred to me to wonder about hating whole countries. It seemed appropriate at the time. There was plenty of evidence that Germans were killing American soldiers, which seemed justification enough for killing them back. The Japanese were clearly evil, having attacked our country without provocation. Our values have changed lately, and we permit ourselves that privilege, while still holding the concept that it's not okay for other countries to do that.

I didn't know about the Holocaust in those days. I'm not sure if I was being protected from the knowledge or if there was general ignorance in America about what was going on in Germany. I embraced wholeheartedly the hatred I was being taught, without feeling the need to seek deeper reasons for it. Everyone was doing it, and I did it too.

We kids played at war, and the boys learned the profiles of German and Japanese warplanes, so they could spot them if they ever went overhead. It was like being in a movie. Life had gotten somewhat more exciting. The emotional content had ratcheted up, and it provided entertainment and, to some extent, meaning in our lives. We knew who were the good guys and the bad guys, and everyone as far as the eye could see agreed with us.

That was my war. I saw blue stars in some house windows and I knew the family had a son who had gone to war. I thought of that family as heroic. I saw gold stars, and knew that that family had a son who had died in the war. I knew that was sad, but I couldn't really feel it. Later, at the end, the pictures of concentration camp inmates and victims started coming out, and I got a sense of something much darker than I had experienced. I was older by then and capable of reacting with horror at the pictures of skeletal zombies that emerged from the end-of-the-war exposing of the camps.

Much later, in the seventies, when I lived in Paris, I saw fist-sized bullet craters in the beautiful stone buildings, and I read the plaques on building walls saying that so-and-so had died on this spot, fighting for the Resistance. I began to grasp what it might be like to live through a war that came to your home. A French friend told me about her war years. She was Jewish, and had been given papers by a local priest showing that she was Catholic. It kept her from being deported to a concentration camp. She described to me how cold she was in winter, since there was no fuel to heat the houses. She said that even now she has to sleep under many blankets, even in summer, so she can feel the weight of the blankets and know that she is not cold. I also noticed that in France when you are served food, you clean your plate. No one leaves a scrap of food at the end of the meal. I attributed that to having lived through years of going hungry. These things leave their mark. It is no surprise to me that Europeans are not eager to start another war. Leaving aside the philosophical implications of starting an unprovoked war in pursuit of a moral goal that seems clear only to some, Europe has lived through two wars that trashed their countries, slaughtered their people, and cost dearly. They know from experience what war does. It's not a video game to them.

CR FOUR

Marriage & Motherhood

I'VE HAD THREE HUSBANDS, EACH as different from one another as they could be.

The first was Dan. He was the one my parents would have expected me to marry. I met him at my parents' country club. We were sitting around the pool and our parents introduced us. He was tall and friendly, excelled at swimming (he was on the then-famous Yale swim team) and was on a success track: Yale Law School, Law Review, a promising future. We would do the Sunday *Times* crossword puzzle together, and we dated in an automatic, this-is-what-they-expect-of-us way. We were a matched pair. Dan went to Yale and I went to Wellesley. We were both smart and our parents knew each other. He was Jewish. He fit the job description perfectly, and for a long time it didn't occur to me to ask any deeper questions of myself. My mother had told me for years, "No one will ever want to marry you." I didn't doubt her. I felt lucky when it turned out that Dan did, after all, want to marry me. Of course I said yes. It's hard to imagine two people less suited to each other.

On the surface Dan and I were a good couple. But Dan was a lawyer and I was an artist. He was orderly, even mathematical by nature, obedient to his parents, respectful of authority, and cool or a little distant emotionally. I was a rebel inside. I hadn't rebelled yet, but it was simmering beneath the surface waiting to emerge. I was also intense and angry and sensual, a lover of beauty who didn't give a damn about the social order and felt hemmed in by its rules. These things were my basic nature but hadn't blossomed yet, and so it wasn't clear to either of us how much trouble was waiting for us if we were to marry.

After Wellesley I was no longer the timid girl from the Bronx. I had a superior education, credentials, and a circle of friends with superior educations and credentials. This was my first break from the implied trajectory of my life—not a major break, but nevertheless different. I moved out of the circles my parents inhabited, where playing golf and cards and collecting proofs of prosperity were major undertakings. I moved into being someone with intellectual pretensions and friends who read and learned and had, at least the men, ambitions for their careers beyond making a living. It was still not generally true of the women I knew, most of whom were satisfied to have marriage and children as their goals.

It was a time, in the early fifties, when even a graduate of an elite women's school was considered a success if she got married as soon as she graduated. On my first day of college the president of Wellesley gave a welcoming speech to the freshman class. She quoted the school's motto: *Non Ministrari sed Ministrare*, which means, "Not to be ministered unto, but to minister." She told the freshman class, the cream of the country's crop of smart girls that year, that it should be translated as "Not to be ministered unto, but to be ministers' wives."

So Dan and I got engaged in my senior year, and he graduated from Yale Law School and moved to Washington to work for a Senate committee. I finished my last year of college and we were married a week after my graduation. I was already having rumblings of doubts about our compatibility, but I did not have the strength or courage to call off the wedding. I wanted to be married, I wanted to get away from home and have a life of my own, and I wanted to have children.

Dan and I lived in Washington, and I took on the life of a young housewife. It was like an exile to me. I was a fish out of water. I wanted to be in New York, to work for a publishing house or a magazine, and to be where there was theater and art. Washington in the fifties was a backwater, not the city it's become. Everyone was either a lawyer or a politician or a wife of one of those. We lived in a vast garden-apartment complex with spacious grounds and low rent, and on weekends I wanted to go out and Dan wanted to stay home. I compared our relationship with the close and open friendship I'd had with my college roommate, and I felt cheated.

Dan was a friendly sort, who loved to be surrounded by friends. His friends became my friends, and I was accepted as though I were a real person, with qualities. I was not, but I could fake it by then. It was one of the friendliest periods of my life, and I enjoyed and treasured the people I knew through him, and still do, though I have not kept up contact with them. When I left Dan I relinquished them to him, considering them his. My relationship skills were still not to the point where I could readily make friends based on who I was.

All the books said to wait a year before having children, and we did. I got pregnant the first time we tried, and I floated down the street when I left the doctor's office, so happy that people stared after me as I passed. Pregnancy was wonderful for me. I felt strong and healthy, and physically warm enough for the first time in my life. I was fascinated by my growing belly and the little moving thing inside of me. Childbirth was a whirlwind—my first baby was born after two and a half hours of labor. My most vivid memory of it is of struggling through morning rush hour traffic to get to the hospital. We made it just in time.

Jonathan's birth changed my life. As it does for almost every mother, my heart opened wide. I began to feel my feelings. I loved and was loved by someone who had never loved anyone else. I was awash in bliss and in the endless anxieties of a new mother. My mother came to help out, and told me I didn't have enough milk to nurse my baby. She said he was crying because he was hungry, and how could I be so cruel as to continue to nurse him? As soon as she left, an experienced friend came over and soothed and reassured me. My baby was an endless delight to me. I had never truly loved before, and for the first time I felt like a whole person. I wasn't, yet, but I was on the road. I settled into that life, not ambitious for anything more.

Of all the lives I have loved in this life, the one I loved the most was being a mother. I started to come alive when Jonathan was born and at last I had someone I could love without limitation, and someone who started out loving me with a clean slate and would love me unconditionally. Jonathan was sunny by nature, and I was often lost in the joy of discovering him and playing with him. I had the good fortune to be a young mother at a time when that was an acceptable and sufficient role even for a highly educated woman, so I didn't feel the frustration of missing out on a career.

It was also a time when a family could live on one income. Prices were lower than now, but also we had far fewer needs in those days. We had one car—it never occurred to us to want two. We got along without a dishwasher, our own laundry machines, and all the electronic gadgets that hadn't been invented yet—cell phones, VCRs, DVD players, CDs (much less iPods), personal computers, and all the little things that are offshoots of those. Our clothing needs were modest, we didn't take expensive trips, toys were simple affairs like balls, blocks, a doll, books—and not that many of them, either. We never gave a thought to planning for college for our children. Mine had cost a few thousand dollars a year. It didn't seem like a big issue. It sounds even to me like I must be talking about the distant past, but this was the fifties—most people living that way then are still alive today. Our life was modest but not in the least deprived. We had no one to keep up with—we were all living like that. Dan, as a recent graduate of Yale Law School, was near the top of the salary ladder for people our age—he had a starting salary of $4,800 a year. When I look at the things people feel they need now, I can feel the pressure they are under to be able to afford the style of living everyone seems to want to be accustomed to.

We waited the prescribed three years—I was still incapable of making my own decisions about life—and I got pregnant again. I was seven months pregnant with Amy when I started to have contractions. The doctor put me to bed, hoping they would stop. I stayed in bed for a few weeks. I don't remember who took care of three-year-old Jonathan. The contractions didn't stop. It turned out that I had an umbilical hernia nobody had known about, and it was irritating my uterus and causing the contractions. On February 10, six weeks before my due date, I went into labor. As it had been the first time, labor was a rushed affair. We dashed to the hospital at full speed, and Amy was born within minutes of our arrival. The nurses tried to delay the birth until the doctor got there, but there was no stopping Amy.

I had hardly dared to hope that my second child would be a girl, and when Amy was born I was overwhelmed by my good fortune. Her birth weight was 4 pounds 11 ounces, and they whisked her away and put her in an incubator. I went to visit her as soon as I could walk, and stood with my hands flat on the glass wall separating us and cried. I did that every moment I could for the first two days. At the same time I was insisting on breastfeeding my new baby, so I had to pump milk for her. The nurses came into my room several times a day and asked me why I didn't just bottle-feed her. I felt I was in a battle to be able to take care of my baby the way I wanted to. Finally, on the third day someone took pity on me and offered to take Amy out of the incubator and move her into my room if I agreed to be in isolation with her: no visitors for ten days. The doctor came to talk to me about it. He sat by my bed and said, "These preemies are delicate. They can go like that!" and he snapped his fingers. Tears began pouring out of my eyes. The doctor stood up abruptly and said, "I have to go now."

The friend who had reassured me about nursing Jonathan came again and comforted me. I gradually got accustomed to having Amy—gradually knew she'd be there all the time.

Where Jonathan was a sunny child, Amy was independent and determined. "I wanna do it by yerSELS!" she would cry. And when told to do something, she would answer, "I AM—I WEEL—I DID!"

Jonathan loved Amy and was tender to her. They got along for the most part—except in the back of the car. I had all the usual difficulties of a young parent (I was still barely out of my teens and didn't know much), but my heart was at peace being a mother. I have come to feel that the best thing that can happen to anyone is to be given the opportunity to love fully, wholeheartedly. For me it was my children, but I guess it could be the poorest of the poor, like Mother Teresa, or a classful of second-graders or a dog. It seems like everyone wants to be loved, and so do I, but I'd much rather love. That's where the nectar is.

One day, when Amy was two, my best friend came to visit. Amy ran out and into her arms. After a long, long hug Amy let go. Eileen said, "She'll never be the first to let go." At that moment I knew in my heart that Amy was mine, and she wouldn't go away.

My life was beautiful, except that I hated it. We bought a house and moved to the best suburbs and I felt that I couldn't breathe. I grew aware of how stifling the life I was living had become, but still I was paralyzed for years, unable to make it better and unable to leave my marriage. I tried until there was nothing left of me, to make it be OK, and then finally, it just wasn't. Dan and I couldn't talk to each other, we wanted totally different lives, and our years together had brought us no closer than strangers. Finally, I went into psychoanalysis. All I wanted was to find the courage to make my own decisions, but I got a lot, lot more.

☙

I talked; the psychiatrist listened. I lay on a couch and he sat behind me. I went five days a week, for six years, with a month off every August. At first I cried for the whole fifty minutes. In fact, I cried for the whole fifty minutes for most of the time that my analysis lasted. I talked about what I thought, what I felt, what I did, what I dreamed. He said a couple of sentences every hour. Gradually, gradually, I began to see patterns. Slowly, imperceptibly, I began to change. I emerged. I felt my feelings. I knew what I thought. I understood why I'd done what I'd done, and why I now did what I did. My voice got louder. My life got happier.

In the last year of analysis I arrived at a breathtaking level of clarity. I could recount my dreams and spend an hour illuminating every aspect of them including the multiple meanings that are common in dreams. I was shining, clear, transparent, and powerful beyond my wildest imaginings, although I was not aware of that. I had become who I truly was. The sad, anxious, and insecure girl didn't go away, but she became part of the whole that is me, and she was, is, OK.

When I hear people talk about some great epiphany they have experienced with nostalgia for the state they were in then, I tell them, You can only go through the door once. You go through the door and you look around and say, "Wow, it's great here!" and then when that feeling fades you think you have lost it. But you're still there. It's just become familiar to you. It's home, and you no longer see it with new eyes. That's where I am. I know that you can't fall away from the clarity once you have been there, but it has become background. I have to pinch myself and remind myself that I am still the person I became in the transformation that psychoanalysis worked on me.

When I finally left Dan, it was horrible, difficult, and wrenching, but at last I felt free. I took the kids with me, and went to graduate school, thinking I'd get a degree in English. Instead, I ended up in the art department, studying painting, my first love. While there, I met Jim, who helped awaken the rebel and the artist in me. He also taught me to be independent and a lot more competent. I was living on $6,000 a year (that was considered money in those days—not a lot, but a living), and my life was full.

ATLANTIC CROSSINGS

THE FIRST TIME I CROSSED *the Atlantic on an ocean liner was on my honeymoon with Dan. The trip was the wedding gift his parents gave us. I was twenty-one. Dan was a few years older but in no way more sophisticated or experienced than I. I had been to hotels with my parents, but this was something more, new and strange and wonderful. Our ship was the* Queen Elizabeth. *It was vast—bigger than a hotel, and elegant in every way. The common areas were spacious and grand. The staircases were wide and curving, like something out of a movie from the thirties. There were at least three restaurants. The restaurants had menus, but in fact, to our amazement, you could order anything you could think of. I'm not sure if there were limits to that, because we were lacking the kind of experience that would let us think of something that would stretch the kitchen's capabilities.*

Even in tourist class you dressed for dinner. It really was like being in a movie. It had an unreal quality to it, simply because what was ordinary and routine to the world of the Atlantic crossing was exotic and glamorous compared to our daily lives.

I made the trip many more times—partly because I was afraid to fly across the ocean and partly because I loved traveling by ship. I once read a quote by someone very smart (I don't remember who) who said, "The pleasure of a voyage by ship begins when you get the brochures. The pleasure of an automobile trip begins when you look at the maps. The pleasure of a train trip begins when you get on the train. The pleasure of a bus trip begins when you look out the window. The pleasure of an airplane trip begins when you get off the plane."

I went back and forth to Europe on the Queen Mary, *the* Parthia, *the* France, *the* United States, *the* Rotterdam, *and another Dutch liner whose name I've forgotten. Later I crossed on the* QEII, *and that time we went first class. I was traveling with Robert, a friend from the past, who served to comfort and succor me for a while until my next life started. The ship crossings offered five or six days of complete change of scene, walks around the deck, swimming pools, three meals, and morning, afternoon, and late-night buffets, in case you got hungry between meals. In the evening there were dances or shows. There was gambling on the* QEII, *and since I was with a Sagittarius—they are famous for loving to gamble—we did that often. (He was the man I fled to when I left Paris, and I loved him not wisely but too well.) He won at blackjack three nights in a row, and after that he walked with a swagger. Of course, first class was impressive and grand, but my favorite crossing was on the* France. *The French have made living an art.*

Now that ocean liners are a thing of the past (cruising is not the same thing), I'm grateful that I had a chance to experience it. It will stay alive in my memory until I die. When the last of my fellow passengers is gone, the ocean crossings and the great ocean liners will pass into history.

ೞ FIVE

Jim

JIM WAS A DIFFERENT KETTLE of fish from Dan. He was a handsome bachelor, silver-haired and blue-eyed and charming. He worked as a systems analyst and lived in a tiny townhouse in Foggy Bottom and drove a robin's egg blue MG. From Jim I learned to expand my horizons so far beyond my upbringing that I became almost unrecognizable to myself. He opened my eyes and taught me to see. I'm thinking of a bed he bought—when I saw it I thought it was unbelievably ugly. An antique Spanish wooden painted bed, so high off the ground you needed a stepstool to climb into it. It was original, wild, funky, decades before the word funky even existed. Gradually I got used to it and came to see how beautiful it was. And the paintings of Milton Avery—when I first saw them I thought them plain and without skill. I learned to see those, too. For an artist my eyes were incredibly limited and upbringing-bound—but not Jim's. I loved him deeply for that. I was, though, one of the few people I knew who loved him. He was far too independent and self-motivated to appeal to many people.

Amy hated him and Jonathan loved him. When my mother met him she told me I shouldn't marry him. "He's too good-looking for you." I didn't realize then that along with the put-down she was warning me that he would attract women, and there would be trouble. I found that out later.

CR

Jim was a ship's captain in his soul. All that he lacked was a boat. After some discussion, he convinced me, and we went in search of one. I saw the boat first in Annapolis. I had never ever even thought about wanting a boat, and here I was taking one for a sail to see if we wanted to buy it. As always, I was being swept into a life I had never dreamed of by Jim's enthusiasms and desires. We sailed around the Chesapeake with the owner that day and Jim demonstrated his lack of expertise at the helm, but nevertheless we bought the boat, a 40-foot yawl with teak decks and a fiberglass hull and room enough for us to live on it for months at a time—I suppose even years at a time, but that never came up.

We sailed the boat up and down the coast that summer, from Maryland to Nantucket and back. Jim got better and better at it—he was clearly a natural sailor. I discovered it was a wonderful way to travel. You pack all your things into the boat and go off on an adventure without ever having to pack and unpack again until you get back. Also, everything looks a lot more beautiful and romantic from a little way off shore than it does when you get there. I was often impatient with the pace of sailboat travel, but for Jim, a true sailor, that was why we were there. Jim transformed into a captain, expecting to be obeyed without argument when he gave an order, and I tried hard to indulge him because that was what he wanted, and besides, as he explained to me, those were the rules. I came home feeling stronger and more physically fit than I ever had in my life.

Jim and I went to France together one summer. It was his first time in Europe and he fell madly in love with it. I could understand that. My first trip there had been on my honeymoon with Dan, and I too was captivated by the everyday beauty of it, the beauty of the houses, the streets, the fields, the shops, the food. Jim's longing reawakened my own, and after we got married we decided to move to Paris. The plan was, we would move there and live on the money we had between us until we could find work. Looking back on it now, it terrifies me to think that I agreed to that. It's a glaring example of how far I had come from who I used to be. The woman who took ten years to leave the husband she couldn't live with was now someone who was leaping off the edge of the cliff into the unknown with hardly a look back.

The rest of the plan was that we would put the sailboat on a freighter like some giant unwieldy package and send it to Europe. We would live in Paris in the winter and sail around the Mediterranean all summer. The astonishing thing is that we did.

∞

We moved to Paris in the early summer of 1969. It is difficult to get into France for a stay of long duration. It is even more difficult to get out. (More on that later.) For us, the entrance ritual involved visits and phone calls to the French consulate in New York, where we eventually received a paper entitling us to a *déménagement ménagère*, that is, we could move our household goods without incurring duty. We sold nearly all our belongings and sailed to Europe on an ocean liner, armed with visas that allowed us to stay in Paris indefinitely.

When we arrived in Paris with the small pile of worldly goods we had brought with us, we were still obliged to go through the customs ritual in order to get all the proper and necessary stamps on our papers. We arrived at a long wooden counter where two uniformed men informed us that it was now the lunch hour, and they would be back in two hours to check us through. We should wait. It was our first glimpse of the sacredness of dining in France.

Our next hurdle was the requesting of identity papers, which needed to be done at the *préfecture* in Paris. Jim and I arrived in all innocence and found ourselves in a horde of foreigners with the same need. We were directed to a line that looked endless, and turned out to move at a glacial pace. It took us two days to arrive at the front of the line. This meant that after the first day we had to get a number identifying us as returning customers, in order not to have to start again at the back of the line, which would have resulted in our never getting to the front, since it was a two-day line.

Eventually we got our papers, and after a stay of a few years I became the proud possessor of a *carte bleue* (also known as a *carte de séjour*), the equivalent of a green card in the U.S. We spent our first weeks in an apartment hotel, and then moved to a sublet apartment on Boulevard Edgar Quinet over Paris's first supermarket—Inno (short for Innovation).

Jim and I spent our time looking for a more permanent place to live and eventually found one in a working-class neighborhood, a tiny apartment with two bedrooms and one closet. I began to have nightmares about fitting our life into the confines of that space. As it turned out, I needn't have worried—we weren't there that long, and we never inhabited that apartment.

After a month or two of living in Paris, my brother called me to tell me my mother had been acting strangely. He didn't know what it meant—thought it might have to do with my leaving and taking her grandchildren away. Then a few days later my father called me in a towering rage—far angrier and more out of control than I had ever heard him. He demanded to know why I hadn't come back yet from France. I said I had no idea I'd been needed, but he didn't hear me. He hung up and I moved into action immediately, getting the three of us—the kids and me—plane reservations and all the necessary paperwork for our departure, including documents attesting to our having been vaccinated for smallpox, a requirement for entry into the U.S. in those days.

My brother met us at the airport and told us my mother was in the hospital with a malignant brain tumor. When I walked into her room I saw that my mother was listless and lethargic, but when she caught sight of me she snapped up in the bed and spoke with the intensity of a volcanic explosion.

"NOW," she said haltingly, staring at me, "NOW—NOW she can begin to—make amends." I went to her and she took my hand. She pushed away anyone else who approached us. The intensity of her gaze was fierce, but those were the last semi-coherent words she spoke. The tumor had robbed her of her speech, and eventually would take her linear thinking, but the communication was overwhelming—far more than I could handle. It has given me a profound distaste for death-bed scenes, and motivated me to live my life so that it is all said before it's time for me to die. It was searingly moving to realize that she wanted an emotional clearing between us, and almost unbearable to know that it had become impossible. I did my best to show her love. I don't know if it helped. It's the most tragic scene I have ever lived.

It became obvious that I couldn't go back to Paris yet. My mother was incapacitated, and my father had a lymphatic cancer that she had not told him about. In those days cancer was a big family secret, and patients were treated like helpless children. It's different now, but when I am a patient I still find myself put in the role of the one who doesn't need explanations because she can't really understand.

Jim came back from Paris, we found an apartment in New York, and I frantically threw myself at the mercy of two of the best private schools in New York, who responded with commendable compassion and accepted Jonathan and Amy two weeks into the semester. My father paid our rent.

Then my father was hospitalized. My mother was released from the hospital to her home in Mount Vernon, and my father was admitted to Mount Sinai at the north end of New York. My father gave me the use of their car, and I visited both of them every day. My brother explained that he did not have a real relationship with either of them, and didn't feel called upon to take care of them. For me that was not the issue. Once you become a mother you also become a daughter—or at least I did, and the idea of abandoning my difficult parents in their hour of need was unthinkable to me.

I commuted from our apartment in lower Manhattan to the top of New York and the Westchester suburbs, and Jim took care of everything else. He kept the household running, took care of the kids, and cooked the meals. I remember coming home from one of my exhausting days to find a beautiful and elaborate meal that he had made for us. The effort to be appreciative was the last straw in my emotional reserves. I felt it as a demand, and I couldn't handle it. I fell apart and blew up and told him I didn't want beautiful food, I just wanted to eat something and go to bed. Jim was horrendously hurt by that, and I think I didn't even have the resources to apologize and comfort him. I am sorry, Jim.

My father was eventually released from the hospital, and I could visit them both at home. We hired a nurse for my mother, who was incapable of taking care of herself, and my father moved into my brother's old bedroom. I spent some time with my mother holding her hand and talking to her, though I was pretty sure she couldn't understand my words. Then I would read to my father, who was by then in a lot of pain. I'm sure he suspected what was happening to him, but we never talked about it. I guess I had neither the courage nor the strength of character to violate the taboos and take things into my own hands to tell him. I wish I had.

When we moved back to New York from Paris we had no idea how long we would need to stay. My father offered to buy us a house near him in Westchester. I'm sure he was nervous that we would abandon him and he'd be alone and sick. But as my mother declined, he also declined. We came back in September, and in November they both died, within ten days of each other. Looking back on that time I see that I was out of my mind with stress, bearing a burden that was simply too heavy for me and under which I continually buckled. However, I managed not to fail my mother or my father, something for which I am eternally grateful. They both died at home, and I suppose that gave them some measure of comfort, though neither death was the conscious letting go that I would choose for myself, if I am given a choice.

To my astonishment, my brother and I inherited a considerable sum of money, enough for each of us to live on. Suddenly our circumstances had changed dramatically for the better. Jim and I stayed in New York, taking care of my parents' estates and waiting out the school year. In June we packed up again and left for Paris, this time with enough money that we knew how we could live.

SAILING THE MEDITERRANEAN

JIM AND I SAILED AROUND *the Mediterranean for three summers.
The first year we sailed from Porto Santo Stefano, in Italy, around
the coast toward France and Spain. My friend Eileen came with
us, and Jonathan, and we hired a crew, a young man from Maine
named Nat who knew boats and wanted a chance to sail in Europe.
Sailing in the Mediterranean wasn't just sailing, as it had been
when we sailed the coast of New England. It was also snorkeling
in blue-green water where you could see the anchor dug into the
sand twenty feet down. It was docking in picturesque Italian and
French towns and visiting them, buying the local cheeses and wines
and the fruits in season and feasting on the deck as we watched the
harbor life. Or it was eating in small local restaurants that served
food whose quality was many rungs up the ladder from the food we'd
eaten in American restaurants. It was visiting the calanques near
Cassis and diving for sea urchins and eating the pink insides, careful
of the black spines dripping the water we'd just pulled them from.*

*The second year we made longer overnight sails and hopped
around the coast to Spain. We sailed to Majorca and then Minorca,
and from there we crossed the Mediterranean to Sardinia. The sea
was dead calm for the entire crossing, and we never raised the sails.
Sea turtles lay on the glassy surface like small rocks. We were surrounded by flat green-blue water from horizon to horizon. Once I
sat at the helm staring around and saw something white shoot up
from the surface of the water in the far distance. As I looked, it happened again. Slowly it dawned on me that it was a whale spouting.
It was the first one I'd ever seen, and it seemed unreal, like a story.
As I watched, it happened a third time, this time nearer. I told Jim,
and we stood and watched it getting closer and closer, spouting as
it came. I was getting more and more excited as it came toward us,
getting more real as it got closer. Suddenly, we could see it, a huge*

dark shape just beneath the surface of the water. I saw its head a few feet from the boat, and then it dove under the boat and came up on the other side. I was over the moon with awe and excitement, and I screamed to Jim. As I came out of my rapture I saw that Jim was stiff with anxiety and just beginning to relax into relief. He told me all he could think of as the whale came toward us was the stories he'd read of whales breaking a boat in two with one flip of their tail. He'd been terrified while I was ecstatic.

Once, on a beach in Hawaii I looked up and saw whales playing far offshore. I felt an irresistible pull and I stood up and ran to the water, pulling off my shirt as I ran. I dashed into the water without pause—something I never did. I always take a gradual approach to getting into the water, getting used to the cold little by little. But I had no time for that now. I had to be in the water with the whales. Distance didn't matter—I could see them! We were in the same water! The connection I felt with those whales seems to me to be of a piece with the joy I felt as the whale came to our boat and let us know he knew we were there.

We got to Sardinia at last, having motored the whole way, much to Jim's disappointment. We pulled in to one of the few anchorages, which happened to be a resort of an elegance I do not often see. The place had just opened, and was already frequented by the beautiful people of Europe. Jim's head was swiveling constantly to see the stunning young girls. We went to dinner in the hotel restaurant that night—I guess arriving in a boat gives you entry into places you might otherwise not be able to aspire to. As we went to dinner we heard a faint clinking sound, and as we stood and watched, a young girl crossed our path wearing a dress made entirely of golden metal disks, rounded-off squares the size of a nickel, linked together with little gold rings in each corner. She wore nothing underneath but her tanned, golden skin—the effect was like a veil that reveals as it hides. As she moved, the dress tinkled and rippled around her. I know there are worlds in which this event would hardly cause a head to turn, but I don't inhabit those worlds, and it created a last-

ing impression in me. I guess the dress was a Paco Rabanne, and all I can say is hats off, if you can do it. I often wonder what it would be like to sit through dinner in one of those dresses.

We sailed to Sicily, where we ate the famous cheese and heeded the warning to beware of robbers. In Corsica we stocked up on thick golden Corsican honey. We visited the tiny Isola del Giglio and climbed to the top of the hill. Then we sailed across to the mainland and tied up in the snug harbor of Anzio, where I saw fresh pasta for the first time, sold in huge bundles in the market. Leaving Anzio, the wind picked up and we debated whether to leave port. I desperately didn't want to, but Jim and Nat were thirsting for adventure. We left the harbor and sailed into a wind that refused to let us make headway. We persisted for a few hours but had gone only a few miles. The wind was getting worse and the sea was picking up alarmingly. I was terrified and wanted to go below, but below is the only place I have ever felt seasick, and feeling seasick was a hair worse than watching what was happening. Jim and Nat made the decision to turn around, a difficult and dangerous maneuver in those conditions. The boat is vulnerable when it's broadside to the waves, and the waves were the biggest I'd seen. To my relief, we got the boat turned around and we headed downwind back to harbor. As we ran before the wind the waves followed us, towering over the stern. I felt small and helpless. Even Jim and Nat were not enjoying themselves. After a while we saw the mouth of the harbor, and realized we'd have to turn broadside again to make it into port. Jim and Nat were alarmed, and my terror had escalated close to panic. We worked together and turned the boat, went past the jetty and turned into the wind. We dropped sail and the boat righted itself. As it did, a cheer went up from the crowd on the jetty. I hadn't seen them before. There were about thirty people standing there. They'd been watching our progress as we approached, and their cheer was one of admiration and relief. I suddenly realized how much danger we'd been in—to my fear was added the anxiety of strangers. I was immensely moved by their concern, and also exultant that we'd done *something that had earned us cheers from a crowd.*

The next summer we went south from Porto Santo Stefano to southern Italy and around the toe and heel of the boot to Yugoslavia. We went to small islands off the coast of Italy, some I had never heard of before. We stopped at the island of Stromboli, where the beaches were black sand, and we watched the volcano pluming sparks at night, like a dying campfire. We went to Capri, and there in the market we bought purple grapes the size of plums. Sailing around the end of Italy we stopped at Bari and Brindisi and then pushed off to Yugoslavia, where we stopped at Dubrovnic. It had a beautiful old town with cobbled streets that were closed to cars—too narrow, and with steps to take you up the slope. The cobbles were laid in beautiful patterns. We went to the market and discovered that there was almost nothing to buy. No straw hats and baskets, no handmade shawls, no embroidered blouses, no tee shirts or work pants. There were almost no objects. I remember the butcher shop though, because at its door hung a freshly skinned lamb carcass, hung by the heels, its tongue sticking out and blood dripping from its mouth. It almost cured me of eating. We did eat, though, that night, in a little restaurant that served fresh fish, simply prepared and simply delicious.

From Dubrovnic we sailed to an island whose name I don't remember. You've never heard of it anyway. There we were stared at by half the town, and we learned that we were the first Americans they had ever seen. I felt that I had come far.

We turned back and rounded the boot again, stopping at a port in southern Italy where the ancient harbor had been carved out of the rock—the jetty and the stanchions were red-brown rock, worn down to rounded forms by centuries of use. There we bought prickly pears in the market, peeled them and ate them and learned why they have that name. Even when the peel is gone there are little prickles in the fruit, and they stick in your tongue and drive you crazy. The fruit is delicious, but it's not worth it.

I'm forever grateful to Jim for all those adventures. I would never have had them without him.

❧ SIX
Back to Paris

O N OUR RETURN WE FOUND an apartment in Paris so surpassingly beautiful it seemed it could only be real in a dream or
a movie. It was actually not expensive, being owned by an old
and venerable insurance company that was one of the best and
most reasonable landlords in Paris. For the same price as our
two bedrooms in Greenwich Village we rented an apartment
on the Boulevard Saint-Germain in the seventh arrondissement, considered the aristocratic neighborhood in Paris. The
apartment had two wings, split by the front entry, which came
in at the middle. It was V-shaped, with three reception rooms
in the front and a suite of bedrooms going back to the right
on one leg of the V and more bedrooms and the kitchen in
the other wing. It was so vast and complicated that I regularly
lost my way in it in the first weeks, and had to stop and figure
out where I was.

The apartment was magnificent. The windows were seven
feet tall, each with a beautiful wrought-iron railing outside it.
The ceilings were thirteen feet high, and decorated with plaster angels and garlands of leaves and fruit. Every room had a
carved marble fireplace, and over the fireplace a gilt-framed

mirror about five feet tall. The floors were old hardwoods in a chevron pattern, and the bathrooms had been modernized by our trusty elephant of a landlord. I was living in splendor beyond my wildest dreams, though I later visited many Paris apartments that made mine look plain. However, we betrayed the bourgeois expectations of our hosts, and turned two of the reception rooms into painting studios, keeping the third as a combined living and dining room. We were in heaven.

There was one fatal flaw in this perfection—only one but it was a killer. It was noise. At first I was too enchanted to notice it, but gradually it came through. Living on Boulevard Saint-Germain, the apartment was witness to the passage of two thousand cars an hour. At my craziest, which took me about a year to attain, I sat at my window and counted them as they went by. I heard from my children that a woman across the street, another American, had thrown a perfume bottle out the window at the head of a street worker, so driven to distraction was she by the accumulated noise of our street. To complete the purgatory, the Métro passed under our building, rumbling through every three minutes until late into the night. One week when Amy went on a skiing trip with her class, I woke regularly in the middle of the night from nightmares of avalanches as the Métro rumbled by.

The climate in Paris is mild compared to here. It was rare for a winter day to be colder than about 27 degrees F. In summer the temperature rarely got above 80. (That is no longer true.) It rarely snowed, but it rained fairly frequently. The skies were often gray. I did not realize how much I missed sunny days until I got back to this country. The beauty of my surroundings seemed to compensate for the lack of sunshine.

Life was suddenly unrecognizable. I was no longer timid and despised, no longer a prisoner of the suburbs, no longer living a life that felt like a prison. Thanks to Jim, I was living a great adventure, one that felt totally in line with the things I cared about. It was all made easier by the fact that I had been an inexplicably adept student in my French class in high school. I memorized vocabulary with ease, and the rules of grammar hardly needed to be explained to me—I just knew them. Now, fifteen years later, I remembered my high school French well enough to navigate my life there. In addition, I'd fallen in love with Europe on my first visit, and having the chance to live in France was like a dream come true. Being an artist in Paris was a lot more like the life I could imagine wanting than anything I had lived before.

When we first decided to move to Paris, I knew I was going to a foreign country, where English was not the language spoken, but I didn't realize that I was moving back twenty years in time. I first began to get glimmers of that when we were moving into the St. Germain apartment, and I had an interview with the dignified and motherly woman who was in charge of rentals. Her courtly manners were impressive and pleasant, but at the same time made me feel nervous and unsure of myself, not just because I was unused to the formality of the framework within which we were operating, but also because I knew that I didn't know the rules, and knew too that violating any of the social formalities I was expected to negotiate would brand me at once a savage. Of course, the French know that we Americans are savages, but I wanted to avoid proving it for as long as I could.

Once we were moved in, Jim and I found ourselves faced with the monumental adventure of filling the apartment with life's little necessities, all at one time, in French. We went to one of the huge department stores in Paris—La Samaritaine, the grande dame of department stores, overlooking the Seine and the Pont Neuf in stately and worldly elegance. The building is impressive, beautiful beyond belief to an American, but inside I can only compare it, in my experience, to Macy's. La Samaritaine had everything. I'm not at all sure that Macy's, even in the days of my childhood, had a vast hardware department, a floor dedicated to tents of all sizes, a completely equipped stationery store, as well as the usual clothes, furniture, linens, kitchen equipment, and of course, an entrance to the Métro.

The tent floor was endlessly amusing, and Jim and I explored the tents out of curiosity, not because we had any intention of camping. But it was irresistible to see a tent, all set up, with three separate bedrooms, or with a dining room—not at all surprising in a French tent—or with its own screened porch. Even more insight into the French way of life was available in the basement hardware department, which stretched the length and breadth of the store. In it were such delightful treasures as beautiful enameled house numbers—little pieces of jewelry to adorn your house front—and tiny hand-drills with narrow points, and handles like a sardine-can opener. There were laundry-hanging bars that attached to the ceiling and came down on a pulley to be filled with wet clothes and then pulled up to hang out of the way. I longed for one when I got back to the U.S., but they are only practical in French apartments with four-meter ceilings.

We pulled ourselves away from the charms of all the objects we were encountering, and went on to buy beds, mattresses, linens, towels, pots and pans, knives, and all the rest. The rule in a French department store in the sixties—still somewhat true, but less—was that you, as a customer, were required to address a professional—a store clerk—with your needs, and to be handed a ticket which he or she wrote up, which you took to the *caisse* and paid for. When you brought back your receipt, you were then entitled to claim your purchase. (I was once roundly scolded by a store clerk for picking up a brass hook and taking it to the *caisse* myself and trying to pay for it. "*Madame*—this is not a SELF-SERVICE!") As we began this lengthy process, someone kindly explained to us that we could collect all our tickets and take them downstairs at the end of our shopping and pay for them all at once at the *grande caisse* in the basement. The store would then put all our purchases together and, since we were buying furniture, deliver them. This French version of efficiency saved us a lot of time until we got downstairs with our pile of tickets. We handed them over to a thin gray man in shirtsleeves with garters, like a clerk out of Dickens. He took the tickets and pulled out his ledger, a long book filled with pages of green and red lines going vertically and horizontally across the page. He slowly and meticulously copied the contents of each ticket into his book with an exquisite italic script, using a dip pen and an inkwell, carefully underlining each line, one by one, down the page, with a long square-sided brass straight-edge. We watched him, hypnotized. What century were we in? Had they never heard of cash registers? During the time I lived in Paris, cash registers arrived, and the little old men with exquisite handwriting were no doubt retired to their well-deserved rest. I missed them, and I didn't.

As long as I lived in France, I never got used to the expectation that when you started a phone conversation with a complete stranger by saying "*Bonjour,*" you didn't just continue on and explain why you had called. The bonjour was taken seriously, as the opening gambit in establishing a courteous exchange between civilized people. Only after you had received your *bonjour* back were you supposed to go on with the business of your call. And it wasn't just "*Bonjour*"— that would never do. It was "*Bonjour, Madame,*" or "*Bonjour, Monsieur,*" and the polite reply came back, "*Bonjour, Madame,*" and then, after a moment's pause, you were free to proceed.

It was the same when you walked into a store. At the bakery or the hardware store or the greengrocer or the cheese store, you first greet the person behind the counter as though they were your cousin.

"*Bonjour, Madame.*"

"*Bonjour, Madame.*"

Okay, now, what do you want? And when you leave, you say, "*Au revoir, Monsieur,*" and if there are a man and a woman in the store, you say, "*Au revoir, Monsieur-dame,*" because everyone is entitled to the greeting. I did get used to that, and I still do it (in English) when I leave a store here in the U.S., and people either don't notice or they think I'm weird. I went back to Paris last year and noticed, with a pang of dismay, that people still say *bonjour*, but the *Madame* or *Monsieur* are no longer required. They are catching up to us. Nevertheless, somehow I never feel as American as I do when I spend time in another country.

The first time I went to a hardware store in my neighborhood I discovered that you could still, in France, buy one nail, one screw, one picture-hanger. There were no bubble-packages of dozens of what you only needed one of. And no matter how small your purchase, you got the full attention of the storeowner until you were finished. I came in that day just after a man who was looking for just the right screw. The clerk climbed stepladders and looked into boxes and suggested various sizes until the right one was found. Then he wrote up the bill by hand, made one of those magical packages from a small square of paper folded just the right way, origami-like, and then he was ready to give his full attention to me. I watched the proceedings impatiently at first, and then realized that I was going to be entitled to the same courtesy whenever I went to buy something, for the rest of my stay in Paris. It turned out to be mostly true.

The reason it wasn't entirely true is that in Paris shops you encounter two kinds of people: artisans and people with more pretensions to social status and education of a certain kind. The artisans own the hardware stores, they do shoe repairs and mend stockings, something you could still get done in Paris in the sixties and early seventies. They paint the walls of your apartment, fix your tires, own little electric shops where you can buy light bulbs and get your lamp repaired. These people are simple and friendly almost without exception. The shopkeepers in the dress stores, furniture stores, antique stores, camera shops are often breathtakingly rude. If tourists stuck to getting their shoes fixed and stockings mended, they'd probably have a better impression of Paris.

I think my most unpleasant encounter, and one that seems typically French to me, happened after I had been living in France for about seven years, and had become quite fluent in the language. I needed something for my camera, and I went to a store half a block from the Champs-Elysées. A young man waited on me, and I told him what I wanted. He asked me to repeat it, and I did. Then he said, "I can't help you. I can't understand you when you speak."

When we arrived there, Paris had one supermarket, Inno. We lived above it for a while on our first attempt to move to Paris, and we shopped there and loved it. It was full of the little ordinary things that make the difference between life in France and life back home. We explored the vast array of cheeses and the variations on cheeses (yogurts, cheese spreads, flavored cheese spreads); French soaps, perfumed like a spring garden; and vegetables in profusion, which we sometimes bought there, but more often bought at the twice-a-week outdoor market that set itself up in front of our apartment. We also quickly learned that we were to bring our own bags, and we equipped ourselves, at Inno, with those wonderful string bags that are tiny and light when empty but expand in increments as they are filled, and end up accommodating a universe of groceries. I never, in my years in Paris, got the hang of filling my bag quickly, and I always found myself at the head of the line fumbling to stuff it, delaying a queue of impatient customers who no doubt knew at a glance that I was not—could not be—French.

I spent most of my time drawing and painting. I took walks around Paris every day, sometimes taking the bus or the Métro to another neighborhood and walking around there. I usually spent an hour or two food shopping, because most of what we ate was bought fresh the same day, from little stores in the neighborhood or from the open-air markets that came to the neighborhood twice a week.

Sometimes I would amuse myself by walking down to the Seine to stroll along the quais and browse the bookstalls, or by wandering the narrow streets between Boulevard Saint-Germain and the river, where I would find tiny boutiques with merchandise from far-off places: India, Africa, Nepal, the Orient. It was enchanting to roam through these stores—a very short trip around the world.

On my last few visits to Paris I noticed that the exotic boutiques are less and less present. They have been replaced by chains—Ted Lapidus, Cacharel, even Timberland. But the window displays are still surpassingly beautiful. A trip to Paris at Christmas is a rare treat. The weather is cold and gray, but the city is festive. The grocery stores are an explosion of decoration. Colorful game birds are hung outside the shops, their wings spread to display their feathers. The *charcuteries* have windows full of patés in complex geometric designs and colors that you want to hang on the wall, not eat.

A half-hour's walk took me to most of the places I liked to visit. From my apartment it was an easy stroll to the Eiffel

Tower, the Seine, the trendy streets of Saint-Germain, and a little further on, the Latin Quarter and the Marais. If I was in a hurry I'd take the Métro. Although it was underground and noisy, the Métro had many virtues. You could get to within four or five blocks of anywhere in Paris with just two or three changes of line. At the large Métro stations there was a wall map with buttons underneath. You pushed the buttons for where you were and where you were going, and the easiest route was illuminated on the map. The maps were easy to read, except for the spots where so many fingers had touched the map that the red spot signifying a Métro stop had been worn away. When I think back now, it reminds me of the statues of Ganesh, the elephant-headed god, in India, where the bronze trunk has been rubbed to a shine by fingers seeking the god's blessings.

The trains ran all day and well into the night. They came on schedule, about every five minutes, except in rush hour, when one would appear almost on the heels of the preceding one. When I first got to Paris the center car was a first-class car. You could buy a first-class ticket, about double the price of second-class travel (forty cents instead of twenty), and you would be almost assured of a seat, even in rush hour. Some Americans I knew got into the first-class carriage with their second-class tickets. They took the chance that the conductor who checked the tickets would not be on their train, and most of the time he wouldn't be. When he did come around and ask for tickets, they would pretend not to speak French. You could usually get away with that. There aren't any first-class carriages anymore. The French are giving up their aristocratic ways.

The buses in Paris were a lot slower than the Métro, and a lot more fun. Certain routes wound through some of the most picturesque streets in Paris, giving you a scenic tour of the city for the price of one bus ticket. Paris is a city where a scenic tour is amply repaid.

It was when we began to get into the rhythm of French life that we learned shopping for food was something done daily, and in the case of bread, three times a day. No self-respecting French person would eat the breakfast baguette for dinner—not even for lunch. Of course, this custom necessitated a bakery on every corner, and indeed, there was. Some bakeries were best at baguettes, some at croissants, and some had big round crusty dark *pains de campagne*—whole-wheat loaves called "country bread." Food became a daily preoccupation in Paris. The abundance of choices of breads, cheeses, fruits, vegetables, and the rest invited consideration and discrimination. It reminds me now of the terrible profusion of cereal boxes on the shelves of American supermarkets.

I would go to the nearby florist shop several times a week to buy a bunch of anemones, my favorite flower. They came in bunches of about six flowers, blue, purple, and red. A bunch cost 1.50 francs (about 30 cents). When I had chosen my flowers the florist would wrap them in paper and hand them to me, saying, *"Elles sont belles."* ("They are beautiful.") I never bought flowers in any florist shop in Paris without being told, *"Elles sont belles"* as they were given to me. It was a lovely part of the ritual.

Of all the food-shopping trips I made daily, I had two favorites. One was the cheese shop. There was one in every neighborhood, and a number of them on the market streets that dotted every *quartier*, never more than a few blocks walk. When I went into a cheese store (*"Bonjour, Monsieur." "Bonjour, Madame."*) I would spend a few moments looking at the array of cheeses in the glass case. Not too long, because the French shoppers had no need to look—they knew all the cheeses, and they knew what goes best with today's lunch and tonight's dinner. For them it was cut and dried, and quick, and it always ended with a Camembert. So I'd pick out a few fabulous-looking cheeses and end with a Camembert. The man behind the counter would ask me politely, "For today? For lunch or for dinner?" and would then press his thumb into cheese to test for ripeness and hand it to me wrapped in a beautiful little wooden box. I never arrived at being blasé about the process. It struck me that he possessed a level of awareness about cheeses that I would never attain, and for his French customers that awareness was part of the necessary service they expected from him. Remember, in the sixties, the choice in an American supermarket was between a block of Velveeta and Kraft slices. Oh, and something cheese-like that you sprayed out of a can.

My other favorite shopping trip was the twice-weekly visit to the open-air market. They are set up along dedicated streets, from one to a few blocks long. The metal pipes that form the skeleton of the booths are generally left in place. The morning of market day the vendors arrive in their little trucks and set up canvas canopies, long tables, and for the cheese and meat, glass cases. There they arrange rows upon rows of beautiful fruits and vegetables. Not only are the wares sumptuous, they are far more delicious than almost any produce you can buy in the U.S. I never figured out if it is the French soil or the climate or some secret about growing things that the French pass on from parents to children but don't share with the rest of the world, but the result is food that makes you think, when you first eat it, that you have never truly eaten food before. My own theory is that eating is an activity that falls into the realm of the sacred in France, and therefore everything about it, from the rules about what to eat with what (and what wine to drink with it) to the growing of the ingredients takes on an attention that partakes of the quality of holiness.

Plump red tomatoes, fat cherries, mangos from Africa, artichokes the size of a newborn baby's head. Peaches whose juice runs down your arm to your elbow when you take a bite. Tiny wild strawberries in little paper baskets. Round and compact Charentais melons, soft and buttery when you put in your spoon, and an order of magnitude more delicious than our cantaloupes. In the fall there are Comice pears that almost melt in your mouth as you eat them, ripe figs, and fresh walnuts, so fresh that after you break the shell you peel the soft skin off the nut, removing all the bitterness and producing a nut of an addictive sweetness. Every fruit and vegetable is eaten in season, and the passage of time is made visible in the changing display of the market.

There also you do not help yourself, unless you are graciously given permission to do so by the person behind the stand. The French take their *métiers* seriously.

That is strikingly evident in the cafés and restaurants. When you are used to the casual performance of waiters and waitresses in the States (most of whom are moonlighting until they get their big break, or act as if they are), you are taken by surprise by the cheeriness and professional attitude of most French waiters. They behave as though this is their career, a time-honored and respected one, and it matters how well they do it.

Jim and I found ourselves in Paris one August, on our first trip to France. Paris in August is empty, and while that can have its delightful aspect—no cars, no noise, no waiting in line for anything—it is also a desolate and deserted feeling. Most restaurants are closed for the month. Many of your favorite neighborhood stores are closed. The places that are usually filled with life—Boulevard Saint-Germain, the Marais, the *quais* along the Seine—are deserted, except for the tourists. No one gets in your way, because almost no one is there.

Searching for a restaurant, we found that the two-star restaurant in the Gare de l'Est was open, and we decided to go. Two stars in Paris is almost a guarantee of a spectacular meal. The stars awarded by the Guide Michelin are graded on a curve, and a star in a "gastronomic" region, such as Paris or Lyon, can weigh twice as much as a star in a two-bit town in the sticks. So we went there in high anticipation. We were still new in town, so we were surprised to see that the restaurant was empty, except for us. A restaurant in a train station would be unlikely to close, even in August, but the customers were all gone to Spain. So we found ourselves the focus of an extremely attentive *maître d'hôtel* and his inexperienced apprentice. The master hovered as his assistant served us. He made sure that everything was done *comme il faut*. The dessert came: wild strawberries topped with *crème fraiche*. The strawberries were piled on a white plate, and the *crème fraiche* was ladled over them by the young and nervous boy. As he drizzled the cream onto our strawberries, his master stood behind him and whispered into his ear, "*Elégance–élégance!*"

Another scene comes to mind, this time in a small, no-account town in the south of France. We went to the local restaurant, of which there were maybe two in town, and sat down to order a meal. The first thing served to us was a carafe of the local wine. Jim poured our glasses, and noticed a crumb of cork floating in his glass. Without a thought, he casually spooned it out and put it on his plate. Immediately there erupted from the kitchen an uproar commensurate with a piece of ceiling dropping on our plates. The waiter and the restaurant owner arrived at our table babbling in French at a rate that far exceeded my capacities at the time. The owner grabbed the carafe with a thousand pardons. The waiter took our offending glasses. They brought back a new carafe and two new glasses, with abject apologies that I could have understood in Serbo-Croat, so eloquent was the body language. They were still apologizing when we finished our meal and left.

One of the wonders of French food is that every region has its own cuisine. We were informed in the south of France that one does not eat *bouillabaisse* more than thirty kilometers from the Mediterranean. I may have gotten the exact mileage wrong, but I'm not far off. So of course, while we were there we made it a point to eat *bouillabaisse* whenever we found it on the menu. *Bouillabaisse* is a fish stew (to make a molehill out of a mountain) with fish and shellfish from the Mediterranean, served in a fragrant white sauce, and with a hot, peppery *rouille* served beside it. We ordered it for the first time in a little town near Toulon. We were staying in a small hotel on the waterfront, and we had dinner at the hotel. The *bouillabaisse* came served on a platter made of a huge curved slab of the trunk of a cork tree. The cork tree grows everywhere there, and we often saw trees that had been harvested, so to speak, with a few slabs of trunk cut away, but enough left to keep the tree from dying.

Regional eating is an adventure in France. It's fun to find that every little town in France has its own local wine, almost always delicious. That is the only way to drink a rosé—somehow rosés imported in bottles are bland and unexciting, but the local rosé, served lightly chilled in a bottle with no label, is a major treat. And it's an event to arrive in a town called Roquefort and find that they have the Roquefort trade sewed up. The cheese is made locally, and the restaurants all serve it as the cheese course. You are not allowed to eat other cheeses when you eat Roquefort in Roquefort—it's a desecration. In Bresse you eat *Poulet de Bresse*—a free-range chicken famous for its flavor. In the Périgord you eat *foie gras*—not *pâté de foie gras*, but the goose liver itself. Now that I know how it's made I don't do that any more, but then I did. Apologies to the geese, but no regrets. In Normandy you order the *pré salé* lamb chops, made from lambs that have dined on the salty grass from the fields near the English Channel, that give the meat its famous taste. You also end your meal with Calvados, the apple brandy made from Normandy's apples. Between courses you practice the *trou Normand*, (*trou* means hole) the pause between courses where you drink a bit of Calvados, to give your palate a rest and aid digestion. In Cognac you drink cognac, of course, but that travels well and you can pretty much enjoy it anywhere. The same is true of champagne, which is made only in the Champagne region of France. It tastes the same in America, but you don't have access to the many tiny vineyards where independent growers make their own champagne, which they are happy to sell to you if you pay them a visit while you're in the neighborhood. Taittinger may be better, but it's not as much fun.

The list of local treats is endless: *nougat* from Montélimar, Gewurtztraminer from Alsace...I'm going to stop now.

I traveled extensively around France during my time there. I can't think of any place that I did not love. The countryside was so beautiful, and the scenery, the architecture, the wines, and the food changed dramatically with every new region. It is, in my opinion, a traveler's paradise. I would find it impossible to single out one thing that I loved above all others.

Back in Paris, Jim and I spent our time painting happily in our luxurious studios. Amy and Jonathan enrolled in the American School of Paris, in a close-in suburb. They were collected and carted there by a school bus that made the rounds of the American-occupied streets and took the students to school. Though I wasn't totally aware of it then, I now feel that their adolescent years, and my experience of those years, were totally blessed by spending them in Paris. They didn't need cars, for one thing, which spared me the agonies of waiting to hear if they'd arrived safely every time they set out to drive somewhere. And the teenagers who arrived in Paris after spending some time in an American high school or junior high reported that their classmates back home had spent their time after school drinking too much and driving around or going to the mall. Jonathan and Amy avoided that trap. They hung around in Paris in their spare time, learning French and absorbing another culture.

୦৪

We'd been living in Paris a few years when Jim came to understand that I would not be able to stay there forever. When my children left, he knew I would leave too. He saw that as the end of our relationship, and he saw it coming. With characteristic efficiency he set about providing for himself. This took the form of starting a clandestine relationship with the wife of the French couple we were friendly with. I found out about it when the husband came to my apartment and told me what was happening. Jim saw this relationship as insurance that he would never have to leave France. He'd be married to a Frenchwoman and he'd be in the social security system. That's the way he described it to me when I confronted him.

The day Jim left me I was devastated and paralyzed. I picked myself up and went to see a Buster Keaton movie at La Pagode, a theater two blocks from my apartment. It was a Japanese pagoda that had been transported stone by stone by the owner of the Bon Marché department store in 1895, to serve as the location for a party his wife was giving. It sat behind a wall, surrounded by an Oriental garden of rare beauty. The original walls of silk and curved roofs and lacquered beams had been preserved, and it was outfitted with theater seats and a screen. Going to a movie there was like taking part in a wonderful fairy tale with its appropriate surroundings. Like walking into *Alice in Wonderland* or *The Secret Garden* or *The Lion, the Witch and the Wardrobe.* I loved it the way people love their dogs.

The movie was the one where Keaton lives in a tiny room, and everything is fitted into the walls and ceiling and unfolds or comes down from the ceiling on pulleys when needed. I laughed my head off, and forgot about Jim. I am still grateful to that magical place for giving me that when I needed it.

It broke my heart to let go of Jim, and it filled me with rage. All night long for ten days I dreamed I was yelling at him and telling him to get out. They were intense, full-throated screams of anger, and after ten days I was cleaned out, and then I met Jacques.

If Dan was everything my parents would have expected and Jim was the opposite, Jacques was so far off the map as to be terra incognita.

STREET SCENES OF PARIS

I CROSS THE STREET FROM *the Madeleine and notice a shop on the corner. It's a rather large shop, with two floors and about triple the floor space of the usual boutiques that line the streets of Paris. I am stopped short by the sight of two spotted jungle cats in the window. Too small for leopards, I'm guessing they are cheetahs or ocelots. They pace up and down in the spacious window, not at all like animals in a zoo. Here they are somehow chic. Stylish cats, showing off in the window of a quintessentially smart shop on one of the best streets in Paris. They are languorous and indifferent, like stunning models on a runway, too conscious of their beauty to take notice of you.*

I am drawn into the shop, which is full of exotic wares from distant parts of the world. There are handmade papers from India and clothes from Afghanistan and caviar from Russia and brass tables and hanging lamps from Morocco and a riot of other temptations: hand-carved furniture, pottery, linens, mirrors, and visiting bronze gods, strangely at ease in this worldly bazaar. I feel I must buy something, so I pick out some drawing books of handmade rice paper and some stationery of paper so roughly made that I am never able to successfully write on it once I get it home. It is beautiful, though.

∞

After a morning of shopping, Jim and I squeeze our way into a café on one of the shopping streets in the sixth arrondissement, hoping for some lunch and a glass of wine before we continue with our errands. It's a café known for its regional wines, and it's packed with French diners. I thread my way through the tables, aiming for the one empty one in the corner. As I go I bump a table and knock over a half-full bottle of red wine onto the lap of the woman sitting there. There is an immediate explosion of activity. I back away as the pro-

~80~

prietor, a fierce woman in a long white apron, runs to the victim and pours over her dress a half-bottle of white wine. She rubs, the two women exclaim, the other patrons watch, and I slink away and sit quietly with Jim. Over and above my humiliation, I am awe-struck that here in France there is a ritual for red wine stains. There is no dithering, no advice proffered—the authority shows up with the authoritative antidote, and a precious white wine is sacrificed to the emergency. Wishing I could crawl under the table, I cast my eyes downward, but absolutely no one is looking at me. The only way to deal with this supreme gaffe is to simply not acknowledge my existence, and this everyone in the restaurant is doing. We stayed for lunch, but it was a long, long lunch.

℃

On her way home from school, Amy got sick in the subway. Realizing that she was about to throw up, she got off at the next stop and just made it to the bin on the wall where you are expected to throw your cancelled Métro tickets. There, as she threw up into the bin, an old man came and held her head. When she was done, he gave her his handkerchief, and left. I have often observed Parisians behaving with outrageous rudeness not only to foreigners, but to each other, but I've also observed that in small domestic crises they are incomparably kind and helpful. In a pinch, they come through. Maybe it's the result of having been through a war together.

℃

I was once visiting Paris when Christo, the artist who wraps large things, had wrapped the Pont Neuf, the oldest bridge in Paris (whose name means "New Bridge"). It was entirely draped in gray billowy cloth. It was July, and exceptionally sunny. Parisians were milling around the Pont Neuf as though it were a party, and smil-ing gaily. I had never seen Parisians behaving that way before, ex-cept on the 14th of July, Bastille Day, when they dance in the streets.

☙ SEVEN

Jacques

WHEN JIM AND I SPLIT up, I moved to a smaller apartment on the Avenue de Breteuil, a few blocks from the Invalides. I thought carefully about whether I wanted to go back to the U.S. at that point, but I felt that I hadn't finished with Paris. We'd been there about three years, and it felt to me like there was more to go. I can't explain it rationally—it was another of those experiences where you get the sense that life is guiding you, and you surrender to the guidance.

My smaller apartment, though less elegant than the first, was still large and spacious, with the same four-meter ceilings embellished with plaster wreaths and a few putti in the corners, a marble fireplace in every room, and my favorite feature, a round living room. Actually it was pie-shaped, having two flat walls—it was a quarter of a pie. It looked out on two smaller streets, a crossroad, so different from the grand boulevard we had inhabited before. On one side was a stately church, and on the other the Avenue de Breteuil, with a wide grassy strip down the middle. In the center of the grassy strip was a garden whose flower displays were changed with the seasons. The garden had its own gardener, who had an underground tool shed that he entered through a decorative wrought-iron entry and steps that took him beneath the grassy mall. When I think about it now I have a hard time believing the effort that went into beautifying that out-of-the-way neighborhood garden. They had simplified the system of growing a succession of plants so that something was in bloom every week of the summer. When the tulip season was over, out came the tulips to be replaced by a display of the next bloom, and the next, and the next—marigolds, lilies, I can't remember them all. The gardener pulled them out and put them in all summer. I watched him out my French windows. The colors were always carefully planned and exquisite. It was a feast for the eyes, but we were not allowed near it. The grass was off-limits to foot traffic. The other regular employee of the garden was a uniformed woman who patrolled up and down the avenue and blew her whistle at you if you trespassed on the grass. The last time I went back, it wasn't like that anymore. The woman with the whistle was gone, and people were sitting on the grass. The little garden was gone too. One step forward, one step back.

A friend called me one day to ask how I was doing. I told her I was really sad. She said, "I'm having a party tonight—why don't you come?" I dressed in velvet pants and an antique linen peasant shirt I'd bought in the flea market and went to her party. When I walked in the door I saw Jacques from across the room, and he saw me. He was a little taller than me and a lot sturdier, with straight, shoulder-length blond hair that fell in his eyes. He had a sweet face, just short of handsome, and he spoke a little English. We spent the evening together and we had dinner the next night and the relationship began. Was I on the rebound? Probably. Did I feel I had to have a man in my life? Yes, but that wasn't the cause of our relationship. When I learned about such things later, it was clear to me that Jacques and I were destined to meet, knew each other from before the beginning, and had old business to wrap up together.

Jacques was Belgian, a Jesuit priest who had just left the church and had come to Paris to get a degree in psychology. He was sweet, gentle, intelligent, and learned, incredibly strong and athletic, and almost exactly my age, forty-three. We got along together seamlessly. We were like old friends, or brother and sister. He came from a family of thirteen children, a dynamic mother, and a father who'd been the editor of a Brussels newspaper and was now dead. I knew his mother had reservations about me—how could she not? She wanted her son to be a priest. But when we met it all melted away, and we loved each other from the start. The whole family welcomed me with open arms, to my great delight, and I spent the years with Jacques basking in the warmth of the embrace of a large and wonderful family.

In the end, our peaceful relationship turned out not to be dynamic enough to hold us together, and Jacques drifted away into his work and I drifted into distance and neglect. I tried to hold on to him, to go with him when he traveled and stay part of his life, but he retreated into his private world, the world of an independent and a loner, territory I knew well but hadn't yet inhabited. The time came when our relationship came apart, with a sudden loud, audible cracking sound, and I knew there was nothing left to do but to leave.

I knew this because for the previous six months, when he touched me—a casual touch of the arm, or taking my hand—it felt like I'd been rubbed with sandpaper. I worried about it; I thought maybe I had some kind of nerve damage, but it didn't make sense, because it wasn't localized. And it was only Jacques' touch that provoked the pain. There was still affection between us, but something was telling me that the relationship was over. I was forty-seven and starting again.

Jacques reacted without surprise—I think he heard the cracking sound too. Without anger and without attempts to fix what was broken, I set about preparing to leave Paris. When I left, Jacques drove me to the airport, and as we pulled into our parking space at Charles de Gaulle, the odometer on the car went to 00000. We both sighed, and I said, *"Je repars à zéro"* ("I start again at zero"), words from the Edith Piaf song, "Non, Je Ne Regrette Rien" ("No, I Regret Nothing").

CHATEAU

I'VE ONLY ONCE BEEN IN *a house that I felt might be too big for me. I love big houses—I like the spacious feel of them, and I cherish a fantasy that I could confine the clutter that seems to surround me to certain rooms, and move out of them to other rooms more orderly and empty, so that I could escape the need to contain the clutter by acts of will and organization. It's sort of like what the hare and the hatter do at the Mad Hatter's tea party, moving on to the next place setting when the old one has outlived its service. So I see myself in a neat and tranquil house, with a few rooms where everything is, and is allowed to stay, out of control. Of course, it would have to be a pretty big house.*

The house I visited in the south of France was more than that. It was a stately chateau built of yellow-gold stone, with ample wings like outstretched arms surrounding a quiet grassy courtyard. The chateau was the home of a friend of mine, and I spent five days there on a fairy-tale visit. It had belonged to her father and was now hers, and she farmed the surrounding acres with the help of a small staff that kept it running while she led her other life, the life of a sophisticated, politically connected journalist in Paris. In her farming life she produced premium fruits and vegetables, which she harvested and sold to the local three-star restaurant. She would deliver the produce from her farm to the back door and then go around to the front for a luxurious and leisurely three-star lunch. (The only thing I can think of in this country to compare to a restaurant's three-star status in France might be winning an Oscar for best actor or actress or movie. But you have to win your three stars every year in France.)

The chateau had seventy-two rooms. Although it felt astonishingly homey and even in places cozy, I could not stretch my imagination to inhabit the whole thing. I had to admit that I was outmatched. I did manage to fully inhabit the part of the chateau I was given for my stay there. I had a magnificent bedroom with a ceiling even higher than the four-meter ceiling of my Paris apartment. The bathroom adjacent to my bedroom was about the size of my present living room, and had a full-sized couch in it. Nothing was pretentious. It was just totally wonderful.

My friend drove me around the countryside to show me the sights. We went to the town of Tarascon, which has an imposing fortress of a chateau on the river that cuts through the town. It's a gray stone building, massive in size and in architecture, thoroughly imposing from the outside. My friend said to me, in a quiet, reflective voice, "Je me vois très bien là dedans." ("I can easily see myself living there."). I was awestruck at the thought. I could no more easily see myself living there than in the Vatican. It told me something about my friend, and also made me reflect that it must have taken living in her seventy-two-room chateau since childhood to give her such an expansive imagination.

CR EIGHT

The Worst Night of My Life

I F DOCTORS HAVE TO BE smart to get into medical school, why are they so dumb?

It was the early sixties, and I was on the birth control pill—the early version of it, a ten-milligram dose. I was having ferocious migraine headaches for the first time in my life, and finally I read in the paper that migraines might be connected to the Pill. I went to see my doctor to ask him about it. His answer: Don't worry about it. It's probably not the Pill causing them, and even if it were, you shouldn't stop taking it. Because, he said—honest to god, he said it—the risk of dying in childbirth in the general population of women is higher than the risks of the Pill. So I shut up and went home, but his answer bugged me and I kept having migraines. Then one day in psychoanalysis I was talking about it and I inadvertently referred to the pills as "the headaches." So I stopped taking them, and the migraines stopped.

I'll skip the doctor who let me play with his fluoroscope machine when I was twelve, and the doctor who took two x-rays of my healthy three-month-old fetus, because I'm assuming that the information wasn't yet available on the dangers of radiation—or that it hadn't filtered down to them yet.

Fast-forward to when I was living in Paris: The English-speaking surgeon at the American Hospital of Paris called it a "sack of potatoes" and said I needed to have my uterus with its contents of fibroids removed. I was planning a trip to the U.S., so I put off the decision until I could get a second opinion from an American doctor. When I did, he said yes, it had to come out. I'm guessing that with better luck I could have encountered a doctor with a different opinion, but that's the way it happened.

When I returned to Paris, I went back to the English-speaking surgeon. (That seemed to be his major qualification in the mind of my own doctor, who sent me to him.) He was brusque and blunt and had little time for me, but I figured I would not have a lot of contact with him, so what difference did it make? (Now I know better.)

I had the operation at the American Hospital of Paris. When I woke up in the recovery room I found that I was paralyzed—I couldn't breathe, couldn't swallow, couldn't speak, couldn't open my eyes, and couldn't move my limbs. People were bustling around me, but I was being treated like an object. Nobody noticed me. I went into a total panic, intense enough that it finally communicated itself to someone, who then did something to restore my breathing. I came out of one hell and into another. By the time I got to my room, I was in an infernal amount of pain. I called for a nurse, who explained to me that they couldn't give me any more pain medicine, because it would be bad for my kidneys. And that was that. Jacques came to see me, looking at me with pity in his eyes. I couldn't bear the weight of his gaze, and asked him to look away. I was in a world apart, and completely unable to exit from its borders even so little as to allow another person's gaze.

I lay in my world of pain. Night came. I managed to fall

asleep, then woke and looked at the clock on my bedside table, wondering if this awful night was almost over. I did that every five minutes, all night. Whenever I looked at the clock, no more than five, six, or seven minutes had passed since the last wakening. I asked over and over for more pain medication, and over and over it was refused.

I stayed in the hospital for ten days. The nurses were wonderful. The French are at their best when you are at your worst. They rally. About halfway through my stay, I looked in a hand mirror and saw that the light in my eyes had gone out. I never knew there was a light in my eyes, but now that it wasn't there its absence was striking.

I went home and spent another three weeks in bed, convalescing. Compared to the experience one has these days with a hysterectomy, my experience was like a horse-and-buggy next to a sports car. Or maybe it was just my doctor. I think of him now as "The Butcher." Who knows what my experience might have been like in someone else's hands?

In the days that followed, I would find myself crying in the Métro or on the street. But the worst of it was the ghoulish dreams I had after the operation. They were beyond nightmares. They were so excruciatingly horrible that I couldn't bear to think about them when I woke up. I had one almost every night for the next four or five years, and then, gradually, only monthly. Ever since my years of psychoanalysis I have had a close and fruitful relationship with my dreams, but all I wanted was to forget these. They featured people, animals, and other creatures doing excruciating things to other creatures. They were vivid and detailed, and I awoke from them in horror and revulsion. I felt each time that I had visited the lowest depths of existence, and all I wanted was to get away, but I couldn't. They stayed with me, they clung to me, they dirtied me and made me ashamed to have them be part of me.

I couldn't talk about them to anyone. It was my dirty secret.

The only one I have allowed myself to remember is a dream I had eight years after the operation, after I had moved back to the States. In it I was looking over the side of the front porch of my house in Mountaindale, New York. Under the porch were three camels that had been skinned alive. They were covered with green pus and were lying there suffering helplessly. They had been left that way intentionally. I felt that the whole surface of my being was being abraded with the rough-edged horror of the scene. I described it to my friend Larry, wrenching the account from the depths of my innards.

Later, I understood. *Chameau*, the French word for camel, is a pejorative term for an unattractive woman—a bit like "cow" in English, but worse. I had a vision of the surgeon talking about me during the operation while I was anesthetized, either referring to me insultingly or just treating me callously, as though I weren't there or didn't matter. (I have since heard confirming stories, that a part of us is fully conscious under anesthesia and remembers and reacts to what is said—surgeons, and patients, take note!) Judging from the intensity of my reaction, I suspect the first, but maybe not. I was suffering, for years, at being treated inhumanely while I was unconscious.

My suspicions were bolstered by my memory of my last visit to the surgeon. I was sitting in his office when a phone call came through from a woman in the south of France, obviously in a panic, asking for the results of her tests. I knew this because I overheard the discussion between the doctor and his nurse. They didn't know I was fluent in French, since we'd always spoken English—that was, after all, the reason he was "qualified" to treat me. I had always taken full advantage of it. He told the nurse to find her folder. After a couple of minutes, with the woman still on hold, the nurse told him she couldn't find it. He picked up the phone and told the woman, in French, that he couldn't give her the results over the phone. She must have asked again, because he said, "No, I can't give you the results over the phone. I'll tell you when you get to Paris." (She apparently had an appointment a few days later.) Then he hung up. I sat there in shock, the hairs on the back of my neck standing up at the thought of what that poor woman must be thinking now—and for nothing! Simply to cover his tracks!

About three months after my revelation, and after doing some mental work aimed at recovery, the nightmares stopped and have never returned.

INCUBUS

PEOPLE VISIT YOU OFTEN WHEN you live in Paris—*people you know, people you used to know, people who know people you know. One of those, a couple in the last category, was visiting me. They were sent by my ex-husband's wife, and we spent a week together pleasantly. When they left, the woman gave me a book. She said it was really intense—about the horrible childhood of the author. I thanked her and took it, and read a couple of chapters when I had time. One night in the middle of deep sleep I dreamed that something dark was hiding behind the curtains in my living room. It began to emerge, frightening me. Suddenly I felt that something scary and sinister was sitting on my chest. I could feel its oppressive presence but I couldn't see it—it was just a dark shape in the dark. I couldn't breathe—the weight of it on my chest was suppressing my breath. I tried to cry out but I couldn't. The effort woke me up, and the thing was still there, and I still couldn't breathe. I was terrified. Gradually my breath came back and the thing was no longer there, but it took hours for my terror to abate.*

The next day I continued reading the book the friend-of-a-friend had given me. A few pages into the next chapter I came to a description of the author's experience with a recurring nightmare. He described having exactly the experience I had had the night before.

I threw the book in the trash and carried the trash out to the trash bin. Jacques wanted to read it, but I wouldn't let him. I couldn't be in the house with that book there.

*Incubus: a demon supposed to be the cause of nightmare (*in: upon; cubare: to lie).

∾ NINE

My Dance with Cancer

YEARS AGO, ON ONE OF my annual checkup visits to what is now called a primary care physician, but was then just my doctor, he found a little lump in my breast. He sent me to a surgeon, who examined me and told me the lump was a cluster of cysts, nothing to worry about. I went away and didn't worry about it for two years. By then I had moved to Paris, still not worrying. Then I started looking in the mirror and seeing something that scared me. I would look at myself and think, "I'm sick." I started writing poems about death. Finally, I decided I should have the lump checked.

A friend who lived in London told me she had a doctor, a surgeon, who she said was the best. I made an appointment to see him. He was a friendly and self-possessed man, mild looking and serious. At his office in Harley Street he took a needle aspiration of the lump and said when the lab tests were done he would call me. I went with my friends to visit their friends in Oxford. They were gracious and welcoming and lived in a charming country cottage with old beams and British heating—that is, you don't heat the house, you heat yourself by wearing thick English wools and standing next to the fire. The next day the surgeon called to say the lump was suspicious and had to be removed for a definitive diagnosis. He said he'd call me the next day, back in London, to set up an appointment. I was calm. My friends and their friends were astonished that I wasn't more upset at the bad news. When the surgeon called me the next day I told him I would go back to the U.S. to have the lump removed. He grew angry and told me they would do radical surgery on me if it turned out to be cancer, and I should do whatever I wanted. I imagined that what he meant by radical was experimental or innovative, and I concluded that he was old-fashioned and disapproving. I told my friends that the doctor had disapproved of me, and I would go back to America for an operation. They knew him better than I did, and said he'd probably talk to me again when he was calmer.

It was as they said. That evening he called me at their flat, in a gentler mood. He explained to me that in the U.S. it was standard treatment for a malignant lump to remove the breast and all the lymph nodes and sometimes even the muscle of the chest wall, a radical and disfiguring and, in his opinion, unnecessary operation. He told me he would remove only the lump and surrounding tissue, and that trials in Europe had shown that the survival rate after this treatment was just as good, maybe better, than after the radical surgery. I went to see him again and found him sympathetic and protective. I put myself in his hands and went back to Paris with a plan to return in a week for the operation.

I was admitted to a vast and decorous old teaching hospital in London, more like a castle than a hospital—not luxurious, but high-ceilinged and tall-windowed and stone-walled. I was cared for by "sisters," nurses dressed like nuns in bonnets with big white wings, who were caring and gentle in their ministrations. Jacques had accompanied me to London, but had to get back to Paris the same morning for a business meeting. He was so eager to be gone that he left the hospital in enough time to catch an earlier plane than the one he was scheduled to take. When I awoke from the anesthesia the surgeon told me that my husband had left before the operation was over, so he'd been unable to tell him the results. He said he wouldn't tell me, because I was groggy from the anesthesia and wouldn't remember what he said. Did he think he could fool me? It was thus that I found out that the lump had been malignant. (I had no trouble remembering that conversation, even now, thirty-four years later.)

The next morning the surgeon sent his young assistant to talk to me. He explained to me gently and factually what I already knew—I had breast cancer. Again, I remained amazingly calm, and thanked him for performing what was obviously a task no one wanted. Later that day my surgeon came to see me. He said he had now done for me everything I needed done. He had removed the cancerous lump and a wide margin of tissue around it. He told me there was no evidence to show that either radiation or chemotherapy would improve my chances for survival, and he counseled me not to do either. He said I could confidently expect to stay cancer-free. I accepted his advice with all my heart.

Had the lump been malignant two years earlier when I first saw a doctor about it? My guess is yes. Should the surgeon have investigated it further, or at least asked for a follow-up? I don't know. My guess is probably. Later, when I was back in Washington, I went to see my doctor, the one who had found the lump. I told him it had turned out to be malignant. His demeanor changed suddenly and radically. You could feel the fear around him, as loud as a sound. He said quickly, "You've come to the wrong doctor." What he meant was, don't sue me. What he meant was, it's not my fault. He was telling me to go away, to go back to the surgeon I'd seen once and tell him my bad news. So I made up some other reason why I'd come to see him—in those days I tried to protect people from themselves—and he calmed down. I never saw him again.

CR

It was now time to leave Paris and go home to the U.S. For some reason the cancer diagnosis didn't frighten me, but it did tip the balance in favor of wanting stability more than adventure. Although I had no home to return to, going back to the U.S. felt like going home. Both my children were now living there, and everyone there spoke English. Though my French had become fluent and easy in my years in Paris and with Jacques, it still required an effort to express myself—not to speak, but to find the words to say what was in my heart. Feeling vulnerable and needy, and like a foreigner, I felt I'd be understood more readily in my own language.

Looking back, my time in France had a quality of unreality, like watching yourself as a character in a wonderful movie. I was living in a place where I was unconcerned by the political scene, and only lightly held by the social expectations that French people lived under. I was an exile, apart from the day-to-day realities of life, speaking a language where I could express the utilitarian demands of life, but not my deepest feelings. The distance this position gave me from my usual immersion in the play of reality was both a boon and a limitation. I fully enjoyed skimming on the surface of life, exempt from the rules imposed on others by my unfamiliarity with the subtleties of the cultural norms, and my ability to escape into pretending I didn't understand French when circumstances pressed in on me.

It was liberating, but it was lonely too. I was always on the fringe of the scene. I would never be taken for French. The closest I came, toward the end of my stay, when my French had become fluent and my accent polished, was to be taken for Dutch. At least I had managed to locate myself in Europe. I was a curiosity in France, an American who spoke French. Now, after seven years, when the full impact of my position hit me, I made the decision to return to America. Unlike France, the U.S. is full of people with foreign accents and faces. There is no homogeneous group to reject them (a few oddballs, but certainly not society as a whole). We are almost all of us foreigners, and we integrate with relative ease into being American. Being an American in Paris was wonderful and exciting for a long time, but it had its limits and eventually it came to an end.

Leaving Paris is not easy. First, because it's so beautiful, and of all the cities I know, the most livable. But on top of that, there is an obstacle course of paper work to be gotten through before you are qualified to leave. When I was finally ready to leave France, after seven-plus years, I learned of the existence of an exit ritual similar to that which I had endured when I first arrived. I had to report to an office where I showed proof that I had paid my taxes (in my case that I didn't owe any, not being French) and then to another office with proof that I had paid my utility bills. All of these offices involved lines and dealing with clerks who were already of the opinion that you were of inferior stuff, and that what you were asking them to do was unreasonable and impossible. As I stood in the line to surrender my hard-won and prized *carte bleue*, that precious identity credential which gave me the right to live in Paris forever, if I so chose, a man entered the office and strode forward. He was tall and slender and elegantly dressed, and he ignored the line and went straight to the desk.

"*Madame*," he said, in the most imperious tone I had ever

heard. Not loud, not rude, just loaded with layers and layers of privilege.

The woman behind the counter snapped to attention.

"*Monsieur*," she replied.

And suddenly I understood what it meant to be an aristocrat. I also grasped in its totality the advantages it conferred. With one word this man had tamed the dragon. He let her know her place and she occupied it meekly and served him. How I would have loved to have the secret while I was living in Paris. But I knew I was not to the manner born. I would never learn what he knew.

When he was done I stepped forward and handed over my *carte bleue*, hanging on to it until the last second, and crying inside. (When Jacques later remarried, I also had to sign away any claim to ask for French citizenship, which I again did with a wrenching ambivalence.) Good-bye to France. I loved you more than you loved me. It was always a barrier between us.

✑ TEN

Home Again (Robert)

I WENT FROM PARIS BACK to Washington. To my relief and delight, my old friend Robert invited me to live with him. We'd been friends for about eighteen years, and I'd loved him chastely since the first time I saw him, when I was pregnant with Amy and I showed up at his Halloween costume party dressed as a kangaroo with a baby in my pouch. I accepted his invitation now with gratitude and with the hope that the relationship would stick. It was wonderful to have somewhere to go and someone to go to when I needed that.

Robert was handsome and outgoing and funny and supremely intelligent and charming—qualities for which I am a sucker. Like the good friend he was, he consulted the best people and found me a doctor in D.C. who would accept me for treatment without insisting that I have radiation or chemotherapy.

I had come to America with names, given to me by a doctor friend of a friend in London, and I went to see Oliver Cope, the grand old man of breast cancer, in Boston. At ninety he was wonderful and human and listened and then spoke, and gave me his blessing for the unconventional road I had chosen. He commented that male doctors were willing to do disfiguring surgery on their women patients, mutilation that they would not accept so easily for themselves or their male patients. Then I went to see the head of the radiology department at Brown University, another friend of the doctor friend from London. He thought it would be better if I had some radiation, but didn't argue with my choice to do nothing. I went back to Washington and put myself in the care of Dr. Gold, the doctor Robert had found for me, who watched over me and encouraged me and accepted me.

A year later I had a small recurrence in the scar of the first operation. Again I chose to do only surgery. I put my faith in my first doctor, Mr. Murley. (He, like all English surgeons, was known as Mister rather than Doctor.)

Robert and I were happy together for a long while, but then I started to get on his nerves. Another of Robert's qualities, one I had overlooked and am not a sucker for, was fastidiousness. I don't even have a clue how to conform to that. I was messy, while he lined his socks up in drawers in neat little balls and had his underwear ironed. It couldn't work. I failed at living up to his standards over and over, until finally he became terminally judgmental and asked me to leave. It was a huge relief to me, and at the same time I was deeply sad about it, because I loved Robert and loved the life we had together. Rejoicing and devastated, I packed up and went to New York.

Looking back at these relationships I can draw the conclusion that I am neither lucky in love nor a good picker. Another way to look at it is that in this lifetime I am finishing up some old karma and lightening my ego load. There is no way to prove which of those is true, and I bounce back and forth between those two interpretations, or rather, I hold them both at once.

Home Again (Robert)

CR

After I left Washington, I asked Dr. Gold for a referral, and he sent me to Dr. Silver, at a famous teaching hospital in New York. The move from Gold to Silver was a big decrease in value, and not in name only. I went to see Dr. Silver, who told me that I had to have a radical mastectomy, removing my breast and all lymph nodes on that side, and the muscles of the chest wall. He said he wouldn't take me on as a patient if I didn't, "because you'll die." Stay away from doctors who try to kill you with their negative thoughts.

I left his office distraught and unable to function. I called Tony, the friend I was staying with in New York. He said, "Go to the coffee shop, I'll be right there." I sat at my table in the coffee shop, unable to stop crying, and in a short time Tony showed up. He gave me the best kind of help. While we talked, his partner, Sheila, was on the phone finding me another doctor. The doctor she found for me was another of those balanced, calm listeners, willing to work with my own intuitive leanings for how to deal with my own body. These doctors are rare, and every time I come across one I count my blessings.

SPIRITUALITY

I NEVER IMAGINED THAT I *was on a spiritual path. In fact I had
no idea that there was a spiritual path. My parents' approach to
spirituality was strictly practical: when we moved to the suburbs
they joined a synagogue, which then became one of the hubs of their
social life. We went occasionally to Friday night services and always
to High Holiday services, though we did not fast on Yom Kippur.
We never talked about God. Synagogue was not about God—it was
about identity. My father's approach to identity was summarized in
the advice he gave me when I was a teenager: "Never trust anyone
who isn't Jewish." It didn't matter to me. I had no idea how to trust
anyone, Jewish or not.*

*The first glimmering of spirituality came to me unrecognized
—a package I was unable to open for another twenty years. It
happened while I was still in college, visiting (my then fiancé) Dan,
in Washington, D.C., where he worked for a Senate committee. We
were in a car with friends, on our way to a popular Italian restaurant
near the Capitol. We were driving through a wrong-side-of-the-
tracks neighborhood when I saw a poster affixed to the brick wall of
a run-down building. It had a picture of a man on it and the name
Swami Muktananda. I thought, what a strange name. That's all.
But the name had entered and registered in my consciousness, and it
never left. Twenty-one years later, when it came back, I recalled it
with ease. Much later I learned that at the time, in 1952, he was a
wandering* saddhu, *not yet a guru.*

*My next opening came while I lived in Washington, after I had
left Dan. I began to see a vibrant blue light somewhere in a corner of
my visual field. It happened over and over, and eventually I asked
my doctor about it. I was having migraines at the time, a result of
being on the pill. My doctor grew alarmed when I described the blue
light, and called for a skull x-ray. Nothing was found. (Well, yes,*

there was a brain.) Years later, after I met Muktananda, I heard him describe the Blue Pearl, a manifestation of spiritual conscious- ness that appears spontaneously, and I recognized it as my blue light.

Having been valued, to the extent that I was ever valued, only for my intelligence, I had built a rigid and unassailable worldview of pragmatic materialism, considering everything that was not de- monstrable by logical means to be mumbo jumbo. It did not occur to me to open to a world beyond the everyday one of things I could see, touch, and think about rationally. Religion looked to me like a kind of mass hysteria, and the concept of God cut no ice with me.

But by the time the Blue Pearl entered my life I was in psycho- analysis, a life-transforming process for me. Toward the end of my analysis I had two dreams that came from the realm of spirituality, not psychology. In the first, I felt my body start to vibrate and to disintegrate into a mass of luminous dots. As they vibrated the dots ceased to have my form and flattened out into a sheet, which became a moving spiral. The spiral wound around and moved out of me and through the screen of the television set into another dimension. When I woke up I could still feel my body vibrating.

The second dream was even more significant, though I didn't realize it at the time. I was lying on the couch taking a nap when I felt a hollow column of sparks shoot up from the bottom of my spine and flow out the top of my head, curving outward like a fountain. The sparks continued to travel up my spine and out the top of my head, even after I woke up. It wasn't until I had met Muktananda, and heard the experiences of other seekers, that I was able to iden- tify this as a classic kundalini *awakening. (The* kundalini *is the spiritual energy that lies coiled at the base of the spine in all of us and must be awakened by a spiritual master when the seeker starts on the spiritual path.) Powerful as these dreams were, they barely opened me to a mind-view beyond the material world I knew. I was well satisfied with my progress toward clarity, and considered it to be all the help I needed to pull myself up out of the miasma of pain and confusion I had inhabited for most of my life.*

Another spiritual opening occurred around 1972, while I was in bed recovering from my hysterectomy. Jacques had rigged up a way for me to call if I needed help. It was a small brass wind chime and it hung over my bed. I was alone in the house, reading The Secret Life of Plants, *a book I found fascinating and mind opening. I came to a passage about the relationship between mind and the material world. The author was proposing that the material world is the product of the mind, and flows from it. For some reason my mind made a leap of logic, and I thought, "Oh, then I chose my parents." At that moment, the wind chime in that windless room dinged once.*

Two things happened to me in that moment. I knew when I heard the sound that it was a message from a plane other than the one I was inhabiting. The knowledge required a major shift in consciousness. The second major shift in consciousness occurred simultaneously: I knew that I was correct, that I had somehow, by some unknown process, chosen my parents, and the configuration of the puzzle of my mind shifted, a kind of four-dimensional shift that rearranged my place in the world and the world's place in me in some indescribable and definitive way. My relationship to my parents and to myself changed permanently. For one thing, I could no longer feel victimized by them.

Two other less seminal but nevertheless memorable things happened while I was living in Paris. I had accompanied Jacques on one of his business trips to the south of France, and driving home (Jacques always drove—he was mad about driving) I suddenly felt an enormously powerful vibration enter my body through the top of my head. It lasted for ten or so seconds, during which I felt shaken to the core of my physical being. When it was over I said, "What was that?"

"What was what?" Jacques asked.

"That vibration. Didn't you feel it?"

"No," he said.

I turned to look back at the long straight road behind us to see if we had passed under any overhead wires, but there were none.

Jacques had been totally untouched by whatever it was that happened to me. I don't know what it was, but I can guess.

The second, similar event happened when we went north of Paris to visit Van Gogh's grave. I loved Van Gogh's paintings more than any other art at the time, and I simply wanted some more contact with him, as well as a pleasant trip outside of Paris. We went to see the church he had painted and then his grave. As I stood at the foot of his grave, I again felt my body permeated by a vibration, this time seeming to come from the earth rather than from above. It felt like it entered every cell of my body. I experienced it as a direct communication from the being whose earthly remains were buried in the ground I stood on. I asked Jacques if he felt it, but again he did not. I was overcome with awe at the directness of the contact I felt had been offered to me.

These events had an impact on my view of life. I was opening to a wider view of the world and existence, as I had previously opened to a broader aesthetic under Jim's influence.

I don't think of Paris as the place to go to have spiritual experiences, but in fact my time in Paris was rich with spiritual awakenings. The most spectacular one occurred at the Paris Opera House, after I'd been living in Paris for about five years.

The Bolshoi opera was making a rare appearance. A friend called to say she'd been able to get four tickets, and would I like to go? All the well-known operas were sold out, but she'd been able to get seats for one that none of us had ever heard of. But it will be wonderful, she assured me. "Ils ont bissé le chœur," *she said in excitement. She had heard that the audience had asked for an encore from the chorus. I was interested.*

It was my first visit to the Paris Opera, and the glamour was impressive. I tried to feel as elegant as everyone else, but I think you have to be born to it. The women in Paris wear their gowns and cloaks with flair unmatched anywhere else. The men are not peacocks—they are only supremely self-confident and smooth. Everyone knows how to behave.

The opera was okay if you love opera. And then the choir sang. They sang in unison, a union so perfect it was as one voice, one voice with a multitude of tones. My first thought was, "So this is what the human voice is about." As they continued, I moved into another space, thinking, "It's the music of the spheres." And then I penetrated the veil of reality, and all time and space disappeared. I ceased to be me and was only a point of awareness. My view was infinite and timeless, undivided, while music happened around me. I stayed suspended in this no time, no space, no identity state until the music stopped, and the world came back.

ᎧᎽ ELEVEN

My Land

"I had a farm in Africa, at the foot of the Ngong Hills."

I KNOW JUST WHAT ISAK DINESEN meant by that. I had a piece of land once, with a house on it, and that land was me and in some way still is, though other people have long since owned it and lived on it.

The land was old, ancient even, and soft, scraped by the glacier to near bedrock, with rolling hills, featureless and self-effacing like old people whose skin has begun to be translucent. My land was translucent, revealing beneath the surface its true being, the Earth Mother who lay along the round hills and suffered us to walk on her body. Living was quiet there—the vibration you find around cities and towns was absent. It didn't have the drama of a place like Hawaii, where the sea comes at you relentlessly, unstoppably, over thousands of miles, and crashes onto the shore, and the liquid earth boils beneath you and sometimes seeps out and down toward the sea, a river of fire. Nor did it have the active spiritual essence of a place like India, where the deities are dancing in the streets, in the temples, in the trees, in the cows, and the people are busy with constant worship. My land was old, lazy, and boring, and I loved it because it made room for me. There was no hurry to make my relationship with it, to tune in and resonate with what it had to offer. It was simply there, would always be there, offering wild blueberries in abundance, sky from horizon to horizon, weeds and flowers and grass and trees and a spring and a brook and snow in winter and wild animals who came by daily like good neighbors.

I bought it for no reason, almost. I needed a place to live, having been kicked out of the house I was living in when my relationship with Robert fell apart. Now I headed to South Fallsburg, in upstate New York, where Muktananda was building his ashram, hoping to find temporary shelter so I could test the waters before jumping in. I had first encountered Muktananda at Wesleyan, where Amy went to college. Her boyfriend at the time, Jack, had a copy of his book, *Play of Consciousness*, and urged me to read it. I was taken with it. Six months before I left Robert, Amy and I had been planning a trip to India to meet Muktananda, when we heard that he was going to be in California on the first leg of a journey in the U.S., so we went to California to check him out. Leaving Robert, I later realized, was the event that cleared my life out so that I could think of going to be with my Guru. I have heard now countless stories of people whose lives came apart shortly after meeting the Guru. *Get rid of everything and follow me.* The poor young rich man in the Bible didn't have the karma to be required to follow his master.

When I arrived in South Fallsburg, there was nothing to rent, but I found a little house for sale for practically nothing, and thought I could buy it and then sell it at the end of the summer if I didn't want to stay. I went to the nearby ashram and spoke to one of the managers about my plans. The ashram was newly acquired and was a construction site, all scaffolds and young men in white painters overalls inside and a sea of mud outside. The manager told me he'd ask one of the construction crew to check out the house and he'd call me. I went back to a friend's apartment in Manhattan to wait.

The answer came the next day: the house was in bad repair and needed to have the foundation shored up—an expensive job with no guarantee of success. But, the manager said, the head of the construction crew had told him they could build me a little house for the same price.

I hung up the phone and paced the apartment anxiously. To calm myself down I picked up a magazine sitting under the telephone. I opened it to an article about the building of a solar house. The article gave the address of the company that sold the plans for building the prototype of the solar house. The next day, the manager of the ashram called me back. "I just picked up a magazine and saw a prototype solar house with plans you can buy. Michael says he can build it for you." It was, of course, the same house. Not a house for practically nothing, but a house for me.

I went back to South Fallsburg to talk some more with the construction crew. Someone offered to show me land for sale in the adjoining towns. I drove around and looked at the surrounding area, which was unbelievably run-down and decaying. The summer trade had left the area and the once-thriving hotels and cottages were now derelict, leaning over and rotting, roofs falling in, beyond reclaiming.

What made me stay? I will never know.

After a day or two of looking around I found myself in the car with a helpful young man from the ashram who was a local resident and knew the area well. We drove a little way from the ashram to a town called Mountaindale, and then up a dirt road to look at some land. I heard myself saying, "This is it." Why? I have no idea. The land was not beautiful. It was covered with scrubby bushes and had nothing much to recommend it but a mediocre view of the hills opposite. I didn't think twice—I went and made an offer for it that day.

The charms of this enchanted place were completely hidden from me at first. I will never understand the process that made that land mine. The illusion that we are in control of our lives had never before or since been laid so bare to me as illusion. I bought the land and built the house, and little by little that place became a magical spot, a place of miracles, a place of peace, a place where everyone who came—friends, family, delivery men, maintenance workers—looked around, pronounced it beautiful, and said they didn't want to leave.

We built the house two thirds of the way up the hill. I terraced the hill in front of the house, cleared the scrubby growth from the slope below, and then left it alone. I discovered over time that the land was crisscrossed with walking paths, that it had hundreds and hundreds of high-bush blueberry bushes, magnificent wild rhododendron bushes with fragrant pink flowers, huge stands of mountain laurel, an old apple orchard, a year-round brook and a natural spring, miles of old stone walls, and woods teeming with wildlife. Deer, foxes, porcupines, groundhogs, possum, skunks, bunnies, once a bear, blue herons, ruffed grouse, hummingbirds, and all the other birds were the inhabitants of the land before I came along. Once I saw a ferret run along the stone wall I was sitting on, pass behind me, and run on away.

Living in a solar house is almost like living outdoors. The weather is part of the house. The sun heats it, clouds cool it off, the first light of dawn awakens it, and the setting sun scorches it and reminds it that another day is gone. The air moves through the house like a breath. Every season has its pattern of windows and doors that can be open, must be opened to keep the house breathing. In the winter, on sunny days the house bakes, and the east and west windows are opened a crack and the frosty air rushes in. The contrast is electrifying.

On the first hot day of spring the high-up windows in the front glass wall can be opened, and you can feel the house sigh as the warm air rushes up and out, followed by cooler air streaming after it. The house looks out, looks out, looks out through its glass wall at the grassy hill in front of it, its lap. Then up and across to a wall of trees that hides the rest of the world, and ends in sky, empty sky. An empty view. The animals come and perform in it sometimes. The blueberry bushes sit around in the grass and pretend they are not people.

Ordinary things happened there, and magical things happened there. After a while, even the ordinary began to taste of the magical.

The first magical thing happened before the house was halfway built. I was standing in the lobby of the ashram with a crowd of people, waiting excitedly for the Guru to walk by on his way to somewhere. I had made an interesting discovery about that phenomenon. Every time he appeared a crowd of people grew, hoping to see him. The excitement was palpable, and I always found myself caught up in it. Then one day, as he came into the ashram restaurant and I stretched to see him, I asked myself, "Why am I so excited to see him? I hardly know him. All these people have been around for years, but I've only been here three weeks. Why do I do this?" And then, as he walked by and I felt my usual rush of joy at seeing him, I got my answer. I felt the love surge in me and I knew that it wasn't about him. His presence had released the love inside of me, had opened me to it, and as he walked by I got to experience the love that is my own core. The joy I felt was not him, but me.

And on this day, as I waited with the others, he walked by and I stood soaking up his presence. He continued for about twenty feet, and then stopped and turned around to face me. "I'm coming to your house," he said. There was silence, and everyone stared at me. Then he walked on and was gone. I was dazed. People began explaining to me that this was unheard of, that he hadn't been to anyone's house in years, outside of India. I began to grasp the scope of the honor and had the pleasure of anticipating it for months, the months that it took to finish my house.

Just before construction began I noticed another small lump in the scar of my lumpectomy. I went to see my doctor in New York, who sent me to the surgeon who was at that time the only one doing lumpectomies in this country. We set a date for the operation and I went home to wait. I was in a dilemma, not knowing whether to proceed with building a house when I was facing another recurrence of cancer. That night, the wife of the head of the ashram crew, herself a member of the close circle around Baba, found Amy, who at that time was in her early twenties, at the back of the ashram, crying. Amy told her the story, and the woman told Baba. (Baba is Hindi for "father," which is what we called our Guru.)

The next day he called us both in to see him. He asked me to tell him what was happening. Then he called for the ashram astrologer and asked him whether it was time for me to die. The astrologer answered no, I would have a long life. Then Baba told us a story about a man who was generous and helpful to people his whole life, and then got sick and was going to die. Baba said, "God Himself came and cured him." He turned to Amy and said, "I'm not going to let her die." Then he turned to me and said, "Keep helping people." Then the *darshan* was over. As usual I had been dumb and frozen during the entire meeting, barely able to answer his questions and dazed when I left. We went to the ashram restaurant, where an Indian friend, curious to know about our meeting with Baba, joined us. I told him what had happened. When I told him the story that Baba had told me of the man cured by God, he stared at me and stared some more. As I looked at him staring at me I burst into tears.

"What is it?" he asked.

I told him, "I just realized he was talking about me."

That meeting marked me. Since then, when I worry about my health, I remember Baba's words: "Keep helping people." I didn't know what he meant at the time, but like so much of the little he said to me, it resonates down through the years.

The surgeon removed the tiny lump in my skin, and also took seven lymph nodes to check for cancer. There was microscopic malignancy in one, which he said did not threaten me or affect my prognosis. He was encouraging, supportive. I felt confident. The minuet with cancer had become a fast waltz, and I still knew the steps. As it turned out, my dance partner didn't visit me again for eight more years.

ᚳ

The ashram building crew began to work on my house as soon as the ashram was finished and ready to be occupied, at the beginning of the summer. Construction work at the ashram always finished on time. Sometimes it meant that people worked around the clock to make sure it was done, but the deadline was never missed. The construction crew were the stars of the ashram—the Knights of the Round Table, in daily contact with Baba and directly doing his work. They came to my land to build my house, and they brought their light with them. Soon after the work had begun I had a dream in which I was looking at the excavated foundation hole. The crew members were standing in the hole like pillars, lined up around the foundation, and I knew that I had been waiting since time began for them to build me a house.

A few weeks into the project Michael, the head of the crew, went to speak to Baba. There had been many delays in those few weeks—equipment breaking down, things not working out as they should. Michael asked Baba's advice. Baba said, "Are you doing the *Guru Gita?*" Michael said no. Baba said, "How could you forget?"

The *Guru Gita,* the "Song of the Guru," is a long chant that was done every morning at the ashram. In it Shiva explains to his consort Parvati the glories of the Guru. It is done in Sanskrit and takes about an hour and a half, including all the other short chants that are done with it, before and after the text. Everyone in the ashram chanted the *Guru Gita* every morning before breakfast. But the construction crew showed up at my house site early every morning, before the hour when the *Guru Gita* ended. After Baba spoke to Michael, the schedule changed. First thing every morning Amy and I went up to the site, and we and the crew set up an altar on the plywood floor of the framed-in house and did the *Guru Gita* together, at breakneck speed. I could hardly follow the Sanskrit at the leisurely pace of the ashram chant—now it was like trying to run a sprint with Olympic athletes, and trying not to fall too far behind. That summer I learned the words, quickly.

The construction problems stopped, and we kept chanting. Gradually the house grew around our little shrine, until we were chanting in a completed house. The building of the house had taken three and a half months. The crew worked on it seven days a week from early morning until dinnertime. As the summer came to an end and the summer visitors left the ashram, we began to prepare for Baba's visit. The day he picked was October 1—a full-moon day, and, coincidentally, Yom Kippur. Someone told me it was considered the most auspicious day of the year.

The inner circle at the ashram swung into action to get my house ready for Baba's visit. I was still very new at this, and had no idea what would be involved. The one task assigned to me was to buy a couch for Baba to sit on. The rest of the workers were responsible for preparing food for everyone, decorating the house with balloons and paper decorations, and providing flower arrangements. Another group made garlands, and someone was in charge of dressing a group of young girls in saris and providing them with painted coconuts to carry on their heads. Baba arrived with hundreds of people from the ashram—the lucky ones. He stepped out of the car and broke a coconut at my front door—a ritual for protecting the house and chasing away bad vibrations. I greeted him at the front door, almost fainting with nervousness.

I was wearing a sari—my first. Someone had spent twenty minutes wrapping me in it—an elaborate procedure involving a long underskirt to which the first folds of the six-foot length of silk were attached, and then winding and winding the endless length of silk until it draped itself gracefully like a garment and was declared more or less secure. In it I moved like a tin soldier and worried ceaselessly that it would come undone.

Baba asked for a tour of the house. Michael led the way, and Amy and I followed. We were included in all of this by necessity, but the more knowledgeable old-timers took over the proceedings, aware of the honor and not eager to give any of the precious moments in Baba's presence away. We got at last to the guest room, a small room under the stairs. Baba asked, "Meditation room?" We were all electrified, realizing in a rush that we had forgotten to plan for a meditation room. No problem, though. Michael simply said, "*Ji, Baba.*" ("Yes, Baba.")

We went back to the living room where Baba sat on the couch I'd bought, and we sat at his feet. The house was as full as a subway at rush hour—there were people all the way up the stairs, people in the glass-walled solarium, and people standing on things to peer in the windows. There was a video crew filming everything, and photographers snapping pictures. Baba sat at ease and gave *darshan* (Sanskrit for "seeing," the coveted privilege of being in the Guru's presence.) We sat at his feet, radiant and ecstatic to be so close for such a long time. Baba spoke in Hindi and his words were translated into English. I envied everyone's enjoyment. I felt as though I had been twisted and wrung into a giant knot and was frozen tight. Eventually I learned that I was always that way when I got close to Baba. I became tongue-tied, forgot everything I wanted to say, and acted like a bird mesmerized by a snake—paralyzed and entranced.

Baba stayed for hours, to the great delight of everyone there. When he left, he put his arm around my waist and walked me to the door. I was longing to put my arm around his waist in return, but I thought it might not be sufficiently respectful, and I didn't, to my everlasting regret.

When Baba drove away and the hundreds of ashramites left, the few of us who were left went back inside. Someone came running up to me and said, "Come see the meditation room. You have to check it out!" We all went there—there were about six of us—and as we walked in the door we all fell to our knees. The spiritual energy in the room (called *shakti* in Sanskrit) was so strong that it swept over us and pulled us to our knees. We sat down to meditate then and there. The room became, in fact, my meditation room—there was no other possible use for it. It was full of Baba's presence, and even the air in the room felt sacred.

Morris and Ida, my
maternal grandparents,
c. 1880s

My father's mother,
c. 1930, on the grounds
of my uncle's hotel, in
New Jersey

Flo and Murray,
my parents

Flo as a fashionable flapper,
before I was born

My brother and me at about ages three and six

At sixteen, on a cross-country train trip out west for girls my age, led by one of my teachers

*Me at around
seventeen*

*My father, Murray,
with his famous smile*

With Dan, my first husband, at our engagement party

When Jonathan was born and I became a mother, I started to come alive.

Amy and Jonathan were always loving to each other—except in the back seat of the car

Amy and me at Rehoboth Beach, in Delaware, where we vacationed each summer

Three generations:
Flo, Amy, and me

In Paris with my Rolleiflex,
inherited from my parents

Jim, my second husband, sailing with Jonathan on board, in the Mediterranean

Our boat, the Matelot (French for "sailor")

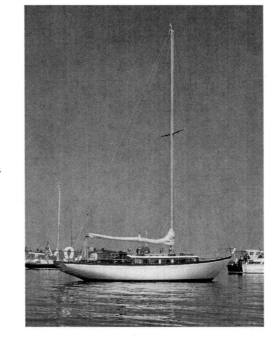

Our first apartment in Paris, on the Boulevard Saint-Germain

The apartment had three reception rooms, so Jim and I used two as our painting studios

La Pagode, the Japanese pagoda turned neighborhood cinema in Paris, where I mended a broken heart

The view from our second apartment, on the Rue Saint François Xavier

Jacques, my third husband

On a visit to Greece with Robert

Amy's house and mine, on the land in Mountaindale, New York, where I lived contentedly for a decade

A passive-solar design, my house reflected the clouds by day and the moon by night

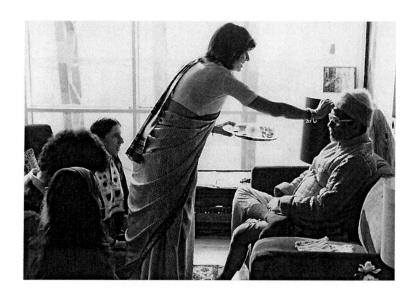

I do puja *(worship) to Baba*

Table set to do the Guru Gita *every morning, before working on the Mountaindale house*

Baba in my living room

Me wearing the key to the golf cart I bought from Baba (he wanted a faster vehicle) and my rudraksha mala (prayer necklace)

The entrance to the ashram in Ganeshpuri, India

Baba giving a talk in the mandap, *against a backdrop of flower garlands*

Brahmins getting ready for the yagna *(fire ceremony). During the ceremony burnt gold, jewels, and other substances (the black material in the tray) are thrown into the fire.*

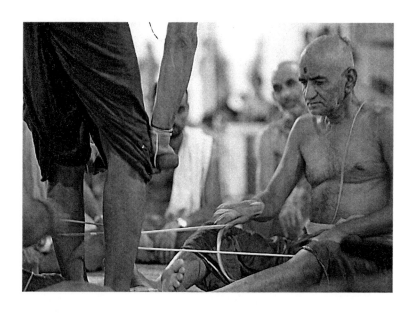

Brahman priests ignite the fire by twisting a wooden stick with rope

Nityananda pouring ghee on the fire

Me, a grandmother at last, with Benjamin

ଔ TWELVE
The Guru

G OD MANIFESTED IN MY LIFE as the Beloved, the Guru—powerful, mysterious, and beyond knowing. The Guru manifested in my life as the Teacher, the Master, light-filled and loving and playful and aloof and frightening and magnetic. I had the experience, like so many of us, of being unable to leave him or even to stay away from him. In his presence I could not look elsewhere—his face drew me and held me there like one hypnotized. I was unable to articulate my thoughts or even to remember them. He played games with me as he did with everyone, sometimes showering me with loving attention, and sometimes not remembering who I was. It didn't occur to me, while he was physically present in his body, to look past the relationship with him to the deeper meaning implied in it. I was too caught up in the *lila*, the drama of the play of being his disciple and longing for more—more than whatever it was I was offered, more than anyone else was getting—so much more, that the yearning I felt would be satisfied and go away. Even now, some thirty years after his departure, the longing remains. I long for a dream of him, and I am envious and offended when I hear that someone else has been granted one.

My relationship with Baba was a gift beyond understanding. Almost from the beginning, he bestowed privileges on me. If I asked for a private *darshan* with him, I always got it. He came twice to my house, a rare occurrence and a blessing. He invited Amy and me to watch him prepare a *bhandara* (feast) in the kitchen of the ashram. Once he came into the ashram restaurant and made *dosas* (Indian pancakes). The first ones, he announced, were for Amy and me.

He treated me like visiting royalty, conferring on me unexpected favors, like seating me up front in the meditation hall, near him, a privilege usually reserved for the important officials of the ashram, the people who worked in close proximity to Baba, and the occasional movie star. He gave me personal advice from time to time, and made me a minor star at the ashram. My favorite boon, however, was the one I received in the *darshan* line. At the end of every evening program, the audience, hundreds of people, would line up in the aisle before Baba's chair and wait their turn to bow at his feet. I loved watching this ritual. As each person came up they would do the usual *pranam*, bowing with forehead touching the floor, and then turn a smiling face up to Baba, hoping to be acknowledged. Baba hit each one on the head with a peacock-feather wand, and occasionally asked someone a question. When I stood in line, as I got to within a few people of the front of the line, I would hear Baba pronounce a full-throated "A-a-a-h." When I got to the foot of his chair he would direct the "A-a-a-h" at me, with a smile. One of the girls whose job it was to stand at the head of the line once said to me, "I always know when you're coming down the line, because he makes that sound." Once he called my name softly—"Elllll-in." My thought when it happened was, "It's like hearing God say your name."

These attentions were astonishing to me. I had no idea

why I was being singled out. It gave me a new experience, though. Instead of being invisible, which was my familiar, and by now comfortable, territory, I was a personage at the ashram, known to all as the woman whose house Baba had inaugurated. It was my first, maybe only, experience of feeling I was someone worthy of recognition.

Once there was a private *darshan* where Baba asked to look at Amy's palm. He held it in his hand and examined it, and then he asked for a pen. Someone handed him a ballpoint pen and he proceeded to redraw the lines on Amy's hand. I watched in a state of wonderment and awe. I felt as though my hair were standing on end. I could not imagine what the consequences would be, but I had no doubt there would be some. When we got home a friend was there, and he immediately took about five pictures of her hand. When the roll of film was developed, none of the five came out. I can't say what that redrawing caused. Amy felt as if Baba was changing her destiny. I have some secret guesses, but I can't talk about them. They are part of my innermost relationship with the Guru.

Like everyone, or almost everyone, in the ashram, I had a great longing to be closer to Baba. I dreamed of cleaning his room, running errands for him, acting as his appointment secretary, anything that would give me daily access to his person. One day, on the *darshan* line, about a month after I had first arrived, he leaned forward as I knelt at his feet. "Will you do Baba's work?" he asked me. My heart leaped. "Oh, yes Baba," I answered, sure that I was about to receive a coveted appointment. He reached out his hand and gave me a *mala*— a string of beads, nine or a multiple of nine. Neck *malas* are worn around the neck and usually have 108 beads. This was a hand *mala*, with eighteen green glass beads. He said, "Do *japa*." *Japa* is the repetition of a mantra, which you do while counting the beads of a *mala*. I held the green beads in my hand. He said, "What is your mantra?" "Guru Om, Baba." He took the *mala* from my hand and fingered the beads one by one. He said, "Do it like this." He chanted "Guru Om, Guru Om," as the beads passed through his fingers. He said the words slowly, softly, trance-like. Then he gave me back the *mala*. I thanked him and left, half disappointed, half elated. I found, over the next few days, that Baba had turned a key and ignited a motor in me that ran by itself. I did *japa* on my *mala* almost constantly. I did hundreds, thousands, maybe millions of mantra repetitions. Hindus and Buddhists consider that mantra repetition confers great benefits. I don't know if I have received any, but I know that *japa* calms my mind and takes its focus away from daily cares, which is benefit enough.

Living in my house, a twelve-minute drive from the ashram, I was part of the life of the ashram, but also separate from it. I went to the evening program every night without fail. The evening program was where Baba gave a nightly talk, chanted with us, and gave *darshan*. The whole ashram showed up for the program. Sometimes that was hundreds of people and on special occasions like *Guru Purnima*, the celebration of the Guru, it could be thousands. The chanting at the ashram was spectacularly beautiful and raised the spiritual energy to a pitch of intensity that felt transformative.

At home I was discovering for the first time the joys of living in the country. It wasn't just the country—I was up a half-mile dirt road, out of sight of any neighbors, in a place where I had the privilege of seeing only grass, trees, and sky from the windows of my house. It was my great joy to take walks around my land, and little by little I made discoveries about what it held. The greatest discovery was the blueberry bushes. They were old—I don't know how old, but many of them were twelve to fifteen feet tall. They bore blueberries in profusion, and the fruit of every bush had a slightly different taste. I spent hours in meditation picking blueberries, communing with my land. The birds feasted, and I feasted, and I froze a winter's supply every year. Wild blueberries have a much denser flavor than cultivated ones. I miss those bushes. I hope they miss me.

☙

At the end of the first summer of Baba's stay at the ashram in the Catskills, most of the summer visitors had left. Baba was going to Miami for the winter, and many members of the ashram staff were already there, preparing the winter ashram for his arrival. There was a small crew of about fifty people remaining, some of whom would be spending the winter at the ashram in the Catskills, and some who would be going to Miami with Baba. With a small group like that, the ashram's strong spiritual atmosphere became even more pronounced, and Baba's presence radiated a power that no doubt had been somewhat absorbed by the two thousand people who were regular summer visitors. I was at home most of the time, attending to my vegetable garden, but I wanted to go to the ashram, hoping to see Baba as he moved around the public spaces. He came out infrequently, though, and it was impossible to know when to go. On this day I decided that I would try.

When I got there, a small crowd of maybe thirty had gathered in the lobby outside his quarters, hoping he would come out. I was sitting with a friend of mine, Helen. We were both trying to be patient, hoping fervently he would appear. After about half an hour Helen said, "I'm going. He's not coming out because I'm here." I was surprised at what she said, and surprised to see her leave. I was not ready to give up. A few minutes later Noni, Baba's attendant, came out, walked across the lobby, and stopped in front of me. "Baba wants to see you in his house," he said. I stood up and followed him, stiff with awe and rapture. When I got inside Baba was sitting at his desk. I went to him and knelt at his feet, *pranaming*. He turned to me and said, "I couldn't call you while she was there." There I was, knee-deep in mystery. He talked to me for a few minutes, and asked me if I had any questions. As usual, my mind was frozen. I did not have the wit to ask him one of the burning spiritual questions the answer to which would put all my doubts to rest. ("Why are we here, Baba?" "What is the meaning of evil? Does it exist?" "Does God answer prayers?") I missed my big chance. Joseph Campbell, visiting a guru in India, was invited to ask a question and asked how, if everything is God's will, it is possible to turn away from evil. Great question. "For you and me it is not possible," said the guru. Great answer. Then the guru told him that was the first question he had asked his guru when he met him. Unfortunately, I am not of that caliber, and will have to wait for another incarnation to get my doubts fixed.

I did ask for some ash from a *yagna*, which Baba instructed Noni to give me (A *yagna* is a fire ceremony, named after the god of fire, Agni.) Then he said, "I like you very much," which finished me, and he gently dismissed me.

From time to time I found out from other people that Baba had talked about me when I wasn't there. It always amazed me to learn that he was thinking of me. The first time I remember was when Chandra told me that Baba had talked to her about me. Chandra ran the ashram kitchen and was the alpha female in the ashram. She was the wife of Michael, who was the head of the ashram carpentry crew and therefore also a person to be reckoned with. Chandra was slim, dark, very attractive, and intense. Vigorous energy radiated from her. It must have taken an enormous capacity for leadership and willpower to run the kitchen to Baba's exacting standards.

Food was a major focus for Baba, who had posted signs in the kitchen and the dining room saying, "Food is God."

What Chandra told me was that Baba had told her to get close to me. In the ashram, when Baba told you to do something, you did it, so Chandra called me the next day and invited Amy and me to come to the ashram and spend the afternoon with her. We went, and there she told me that Baba had instructed her to get to know me. I had no idea why—I still don't—but I was overjoyed at the implied attention from Baba, something all of us always craved. We walked around the grounds of the ashram together, visited her room, talked, and then ended up, at her request, spending the rest of the time taking pictures of her.

There was never a follow-up.

The next time I heard that Baba had mentioned me was again from Chandra. She told me that Baba had told her I was *garib*. That night at dinner I asked an Indian friend what it meant. He asked me why I wanted to know, and I told him Baba had called me that. He was visibly shaken, and reluctant to translate it for me. Finally he found a word, and said it meant tame. He said it was a word you might use about a cow—*garib*, or harmless. I had a hard time imagining that Baba had meant it as an insult, given the context of his previous words to Chandra. Finally, my friend, after an evident struggle with himself, said he could see that that might be something desirable to be—maybe Baba had meant humble, or without ego. He seemed satisfied with that. I didn't much care. It meant the world to me that Baba had spoken my name. That was enough.

It happened once more, when I was in Hawaii. The wife of the couple I was visiting, Tara, told me that Baba had told her I was Laxmi, the goddess of compassion and abundance. Again, it was a mystery to me what Baba had meant by his words, but the fact that he had spoken about me to Tara was like Christmas in July, a totally unexpected gift that I savored, and still savor, so many years after he has gone.

❧ THIRTEEN

Healing with Bach Flowers

IN 1981, AT BABA'S SUGGESTION, Amy was working in the ashram kitchen. It was hard work, with long hours, and was very
demanding because it was considered one of the more important jobs in the ashram. Consequently, the work was done
with great meticulousness and intensity. The kitchen was fast-
paced and perfectionist, and the pressure constant. A friend
once described to me being bawled out by her supervisor for
nicking a clove of garlic as she peeled it.

One day, as Amy was doing her work, her shoulder dislo-
cated. Amy is loose-jointed, and that had happened before.
It's painful, but the panic it provokes in her is even worse. As
she stood there shaking and crying, the ashram nurse came to
the kitchen and gave her Rescue Remedy, the cure-all remedy
of the Bach Flower repertoire. Amy told me that immediately
after taking it her arm slid back into its socket, with no effort.
We were both impressed with that healing.

Two years later I recalled the incident when I learned
that a six-month training course in becoming a Bach Flower
Counselor was being offered in New York City. I decided to
check it out, thinking it would be wonderful to be the agent of

healing like the one Amy had experienced. There was a one-day introductory workshop, and I signed up, telling Amy, "If I'm impressed with the people, I'll take the course."

The introduction to the Bach Flowers was fascinating, and I was impressed with the people, who all seemed light, intelligent, and sincere. I enrolled in the course, which was held on weekends, two days a month. I traveled down to New York from the Catskills and stayed with my friend Charles, a fellow devotee, who had an apartment in a wonderful building on Central Park West.

The Bach Flowers are still little known in this country, though their fame is spreading, and there are now numerous imitators with their own systems of flower healing. Dr. Edward Bach was a physician in England who practiced in the 1910s and 20s. After some years, he became dissatisfied with the allopathic medical model, feeling that it sometimes did more harm than good. He gave up his practice and began to study homeopathy. He excelled in this, inventing seven nosodes, or homeopathic vaccines. Eventually even homeopathy failed to satisfy him, though, and he gave up a successful practice in London and went to Wales in search of a new method of healing whose principles he had already formulated. His intention was to create a system of healing that did not use any poisons (as homeopathy does, though in microscopic quantities) or invasive interventions like those of allopathic medicine.

The heart of Bach's healing philosophy is the belief that illness and *dis-ease* are caused by conflict between an individual's personality and the higher self. His approach to healing was to treat not the illness or the symptoms but the individual, whose individual reactions to being ill Dr. Bach observed closely. He believed that the way a person experiences their ill health or obstacles in their lives is the key to how they can heal. For example, a person who reacts to illness with impatience and anger needs a different kind of healing from one whose reaction is discouragement or despair, even though the physical symptoms may be the same. Over his years in Wales he formulated a system of thirty-eight emotional or psychological states, whose remedies he was able to find in the world of nature. He had an extreme sensitivity to the healing vibrations of plants, and he formulated his remedies in accordance with his intuitive understanding of the healing powers in flowers and trees.

The remedies address such states as impatience, nostalgia for the past, jealousy and envy, lack of self-confidence, perfectionism, and many more. The remedy bottles contain water that has been infused with the healing vibration of the flower whose name it bears, and brandy as a preservative. The remedies are without contraindications or side effects, and can do no harm. The wrong remedy simply doesn't work. The right remedy can have amazing and far-reaching effects.

During the training program we were expected to do at least one consultation every month. For my first one I enlisted the help of my old friend Larry. Within a few days of that first consultation, I saw my first dramatic healing. Larry had had an eczema rash on his face for six months, and had been unable to get rid of it. To both our amazement, the rash cleared up and never came back. I was well satisfied, and determined to stay with this new healing system and learn to use it.

In my learning career there have been a few skills that came so easily to me that it felt as though I already knew them. Spelling and grammar was an early example, French was another (I hardly had to work at learning the grammar and vocabulary). And the Bach Flowers turned out to be like that. My feeling was confirmed when I learned that Dr. Bach's book about the remedies, *The Twelve Healers*, was originally published in February 1931, the month and year of my birth.

"Oh," I thought, "we are twins."

At the end of the training program I began to practice in New York City every other weekend. Larry found me a sumptuous office overlooking Central Park that belonged to an agency he worked for, and which was incredibly inexpensive because it was unused on weekends. I began seeing extremely gratifying results; about ninety percent of my clients were helped by the Bach Flower intervention.

I'm aware that for many people a system of healing that is based on the vibrations of flowers can only be something from the lunatic fringe, but some of the healings I've witnessed are concrete and dramatic. After Larry's recovery from eczema, I enlisted a neighbor so I could do a consultation for my next class. She had been plagued by years of extremely rapid heartbeat that sent her frequently to the hospital. After her consultation, she never had another episode of tachycardia. That healing lasted for years, and as far as I know, the tachycardia has not recurred.

A few years ago Larry, who became a believer following his own experience, called me in a state of near panic. One of his closest friends was in the hospital and had been there for several weeks. "I'm afraid he's dying," Larry said. He was suffering from ulcerative colitis, which was causing internal bleeding that the doctors had been unable to stop. They had used all their medicines in vain, and his condition was worsening. I made up a remedy and sent it to Larry, who brought it to him. The next day Larry called me.

"He's out of the hospital," he said.

I asked him what the doctors said.

"They say the medicines finally kicked in."

We both roared with laughter, knowing that was a response I frequently encountered after a healing. (Larry once asked me, "Why isn't there a line nine miles long outside your door?" The answer is, people don't believe it.)

Later, I began offering consultations to the members of my cohousing community. Those who accept the offer usually do so for their children. The first one I did was for a little girl who was usually seen around the community crying. She had had a difficult and prolonged birth, and had lived her first few years in a state of unhappiness. I was convinced the difficult birth had something to do with it. I did a consultation with her mother, as I always do with children under fourteen or fifteen, an age at which I feel they are beginning to be capable of self-reflection.

Several days after giving her a remedy, her mother saw me around the community and stopped me. She said joyously, "I've got my daughter back. It's a miracle!" She didn't explain further, but I knew what she meant. When I saw her daughter she was in an entirely different state: smiling and laughing, light and bright, where before she had been under a cloud of unhappiness.

The most dramatic result I've ever experienced was with a woman outside the community, a friend of someone who lived there, who came to me about her four-year-old son. She told me he had a congenital disorder that created imbalances in his hormones and required him to be on constant medication. She said he was hypersensitive since he was a baby and experienced "tremendous fear." She also described a level of behavioral rigidity that had resulted in controlling the whole family. And now, she said, he was having explosive behavioral episodes.

That was the most demanding case I had ever dealt with. I did what I could to create a remedy that addressed the conditions she described, and gave it to her hopefully. About two weeks later, just before Christmas, the mother left a message on my answering machine that I preserved and will always treasure. She said in a voice filled with emotion, "A totally new child has been born." She said he had undergone a continuing transformation and was now "so easygoing," adding, "This is the best Christmas present I ever had."

I feel privileged to have served as the conduit for healings like these. As a result of what I have witnessed, I have total faith in Dr. Bach's healing system. I have witnessed a few failures—maybe five or six out of hundreds—but considering the harmlessness of the method, I am content. My healing practice, together with my writing, painting, and being a mother and grandmother, has given meaning and joy to my life. Spiritual growth is in the same category, but I think of it differently. I think of it not as a part of my life, but as my life.

UFO

IN THE SUMMER IN THE *Catskills the roads get crowded with tourists vacationing in the country to escape the heat of the city, but in winter the place where we lived was under-populated and empty. One night, Amy and I went to a movie in Middletown, about twenty minutes closer to New York City than our home. When we came out of the movie it was dark and the parking lot was deserted. I was zipping my jacket against the cold, and as I slid the zipper up toward my chin I raised my head. There in the sky above me was a huge black shape sliding past silently. It was not very high—my guess is about four stories off the ground. It was round and vast— maybe the size of a football field. There were two rows of lights blinking around its perimeter—a red row that went clockwise and a white row that went counterclockwise. It glided past us without noise, slowly, like a blimp. I stared with my mouth open, and then said, "What the fuck is that?" Amy saw it, and we both stood and gaped as it passed.*

Then a sporty car screeched to a stop in front of us in the empty parking lot, and a young man jumped out and yelled, "What IS that?"

I said, "Looks like a UFO to me."

He shouted, "I've been following it for miles. It doesn't move like any plane I've ever seen. It moved along slowly like that, and suddenly it made a right-angle turn. Planes can't do that!"

I agreed with him.

He looked at us, and then suddenly jumped back in his car and called, "If they're taking anyone, they're taking me!" and he screeched off again.

Amy and I looked at each other. I said, "We could chase it too."
She said, "Why not?"

We jumped in our car and took off in the direction the thing was taking. It was still visible in the distant sky, and we tried to find straight roads to take us toward it, but we didn't know the area well enough and we soon gave up. When we got home Amy called the Middletown police and asked if any UFO sightings had been reported.

"Oh yes," said the policeman. "People have been calling about it all evening. But it's not a UFO—it's a plane from Stewart Air Force Base."

"Ri-i-i-ght," said Amy, and hung up.

Later we learned that the area around Middletown is famous for UFO sightings.

ೞ FOURTEEN

Experience Talks

THE EVENING PROGRAM AT THE ashram, a nightly event, started at five p.m. with the chanting of the *arati*, the Indian chant in praise of a guru or deity. The chant was followed by a talk given by one of the swamis or an ashramite. The swamis often imparted wisdom or explained scriptures, and the ashramites recounted their experiences at the ashram or with Baba. They tended to be marvelous tales that inspired fierce jealousy in me, but also inspired me. Two come to mind: the first, by a young man telling of his experience as a chopper in the ashram kitchen. Baba often visited the kitchen, especially when there was a *bhandara*—a feast, usually celebrating a holiday. On the occasion the young man was speaking about, Baba was showing him the right way to chop carrots. Baba held the knife and sliced the carrots the way experienced cooks do: chop, chop, chop, and in a flash it was done. Baba said: "Twenty-seven pieces—count them."

The young man counted them and found twenty-six. This presented a serious dilemma, because it was just about unthinkable to contradict Baba. However, it was even more unthinkable to lie to him, so the poor young man, trembling, said, "Twenty-six, Baba."

"Turn over the knife," said Baba.

He did, and on the other side was the twenty-seventh carrot slice. This story delighted me. An accumulation of stories of little incidents like that served to increase my faith in the power of the Guru, and that faith sped along my spiritual development.

The second story was told by a woman who had been with Baba during his first tour of America, several years before I had met him. They were in San Francisco, and Baba was to give a talk to a large crowd at the Cow Palace. She was assigned to wait outside Baba's door and accompany him to the hall. Everyone else left early, and she was alone with Baba. Waiting for Baba to emerge, she grew increasingly nervous, as the time for his talk approached and then passed. By the time everyone got back she was distraught at the idea that she had participated in Baba missing this important occasion. Then someone described to her the wonderful talk Baba had given.

"What are you talking about—he's still in his room!" she said.

"No, he can't be. He came to the Cow Palace and gave his talk," replied the other.

So she continued to sit there, she told us, and eventually Baba came out of his room, behaving as though nothing unusual had happened, and proceeded with his daily activities. There is a name for this phenomenon—bilocation. I am not personally acquainted with anyone else who's been known to do it.

A third story was told by one of the men at the ashram. He was one of those responsible for preparing the trunks that were being readied to be shipped to India on the occasion of Baba's return there. Many ashram possessions were being packed up and shipped before the day of departure. There were two of them in the packing room, struggling to get the objects they'd been assigned to fit in the trunk they'd been told to pack. They packed and unpacked, trying many different approaches, but couldn't get everything to fit. As they were struggling, Baba appeared at the door. He greeted them, watched for a few minutes, and then left, and they resumed. This time, everything fell into place without effort, and they were done.

It would be hard to adequately describe how it feels to live under the broad umbrella of a being who inspires such faith in his or her followers. You feel taken care of in a way that I think we all long to feel. The world seemed to make sense in a way it never did to me before. I never got that feeling of safety from my mother, though I'm aware that others did experience that when they were babies. With Muktananda, we all had the feeling that he had a power over the ordinary world that made us feel protected from the usual anxieties that life entails.

So the "experience talks" that were part of every evening program were an important aspect of ashram life. Toward the end of the talk, Baba would come in from the back of the hall, walk down the middle aisle separating the men from the women, and take his place in the chair set on a platform at the front. Since we all sat on the floor and the hall floor rose from front to back like a theater, we could all see him. Every evening Baba gave a talk, usually about forty-five minutes long. After the talk there was a *darshan* line, where everyone could line up in the aisle and wait for their turn to greet Baba. The line proceeded forward slowly. When you got to the front, you stepped forward, *pranamed* to Baba (knees on the floor, forehead leaning forward to touch the floor at his feet), hoping he would notice you and smile or say something or, best of all, call you up to him for a brief conversation. Many of us were addicted to watching the *darshan* line, and wouldn't leave for supper until everyone had been up.

It was the end of an evening program toward the end of summer in 1981. The usual diehards were sitting in the hall. The *darshan* line ended, and Baba called Swami Nityananda forward.

I first knew Swami Nityananda when he was a young man of fifteen or sixteen, named Subash. He was the son of an Indian couple who were said to be Baba's first devotees. When Baba was an unknown *saddhu* (a wandering holy man) he ended up in Bombay, where Subash's father owned a restaurant. Recognizing the power of the young *saddhu*, who was then just a skinny holy man traveling on foot around India, the family undertook to feed him and take care of his needs. This is a common act of devotion in India, where yogis roam the countryside with no possessions and are fed by people they encounter who fill their begging bowls with food. Subash's parents and their four children were devoted to Baba, and when he created his ashram in Ganeshpuri they were early and frequent visitors. The children were brought up under his eye, and when he started on his second world tour, the two eldest joined him. Malti, Subash's older sister, became Baba's translator. She said she had to learn English very fast.

On this night Subash gave the experience talk. His subject was the Guru. He talked about Baba with such devotion and with so much understanding of the relationship between guru and disciple that I was struck and saw in him someone who had a rare spiritual attainment. I turned to Amy, who was sitting next to me, and said, "He's the next Guru." The thought had come into my mind fully formed, like an apple dropped into a lap.

Earlier that year Subash had taken *sannyas*—that is, became a swami, renouncing the world and dedicating his life to God. Along with the other men at the ceremony, he had his head shaved and donned orange robes, which would be his dress from then on. At the end of the long and private ceremony Baba invited them to his room, and calling each one in turn up to him, whispered a powerful mantra in his ear and gave them each a new name, to indicate that they were beginning a new life. To everyone's astonishment, Baba gave Subash the name of his own much-revered guru, Nityananda.

When Baba called him up to the front of the hall that summer night after the evening program, Swami Nityananda bowed at his feet. Baba reached over, slapped him on the back, and announced that he was designating Nityananda to be his successor. The people in the hall were stunned. At first there was silence, and then the onlookers went into a state of noisy shock. No one had expected this. After a few minutes of initial paralysis I was delighted, but I could hear people behind me crying and wailing. Later I was told that one of the crying women, a long-time devotee of Baba's, was freaking out because she was sure that Baba was saying he was getting ready to leave his body. I dismissed the reaction as hysterics, but it later turned out she was right.

CR

In October of that year Baba left for India. The ashram chartered a 747 and as many of us as could go accompanied him. For weeks before we left, Amy and I made lists of things to bring, questioning the old-timers daily about what to expect in India. We were each allowed a trunkful of stuff, and the advice we got went like this:

Don't bring clothes—get them there. Nothing you own will be appropriate for wearing in that climate, and anything you bring will be ruined. (Dirt, laundry, heat, whatever—we didn't question too closely, we just obeyed.) Bring tissues, toilet paper, soap, toothbrushes and toothpaste, shampoo, and so on—they are either not available there or are so different as to be unrecognizable. If you like chocolate, bring it. If you crave any foods and would miss them terribly (crackers, peanut butter...), bring them. Bring writing paper, pens and pencils, books; in sum, the little necessities of life we take for granted.

We crammed our trunks full to the brim and set off for a stay of a few months. That first year Amy and I stayed for five months. The trip was arduous—a seventeen-hour plane ride, whose only relief was a stopover in London, Bahrain, or Frankfurt. (Stopping in London on the way to India, we would load up on Cadbury's chocolate, which we brought for ourselves and as treasured gifts for our friends who were there.) As a result, I planned to go only when we could stay for a few months at a time. I didn't want to be in India during the hot summer months—the cold winter months were already more heat than I could bear—and I didn't want to be there during monsoon, when travel was considered inadvisable, and the dirt roads turned to mud and the ditches to rivers and the fields around the ashram filled with water and unsavory creatures.

○ﾟ FIFTEEN

India

THE CHARTERED PLANE CARRYING BABA and his ashramites,
including Amy and me, landed in Bombay early on an
October morning in 1981. Later I learned that planes in India
routinely took off and landed in the cool, pre-dawn hours,
because in the daytime heat the air is too thin to support the
flight of a commercial airliner.

Muktananda's guru, Bhagawan Nityananda, had built his
ashram in Ganeshpuri, a tiny town a few hours' heart-stopping
drive north of Bombay. When he left his guru to become one
himself, Muktananda walked up the dusty road about a mile,
and built an ashram in a spot that was nothing more than a
wide place in the road. The ashram grew gradually over the
years, and when I arrived it was home to hundreds of Western
seekers and Indian devotees.

Buses from the ashram met us at the airport, and after
going through a demanding customs process in the terminal,
we began our journey through the streets of Bombay, heading
north. We passed metal-roofed shantytowns, with tiny shacks
crowded one beside the other as far as I could see. It was the
hour of getting ready for the day, and many Indians were

squatting by the side of the road. At first I thought they were waiting for a bus or for a friend, but soon I realized that they were doing what we call going to the bathroom—clearly, not a universally accurate description. I was taken aback by the difference in habits I was encountering. I'd been prepared to find an exotic foreign culture, but I just never got accustomed to how exotic, how foreign India could be.

As we left Bombay we got onto a main commercial road going north. It was a two-lane road, packed to capacity with trucks and a few cars and buses like ours. We entered a chaotic stream of Indian rush-hour traffic driving on the "wrong" side of the road, which is always enough to unnerve me in the best of circumstances. The first thing I noticed on the road was the heavy use of horns. Trucks, cars, and buses heading toward each other at unreal speeds left long traces of horn blasts in the air as they went. I don't know what purpose it served—it was impossible for them not to see each other as they approached each other head-on, traveling a road that barely allowed two vehicles abreast.

The second thing I noticed was that the trucks were decorated as though they were exhibits in some funky folk-art gallery. They were painted in bright colors and decorated in front with fringes or garlands hanging from the roof. They had images of gods, and painted eyes, and silvery things hanging from the rear-view mirror in front of the driver. They had words painted on them, especially in the back. My favorite was "HONK OK" on the left side and "PLEASE" on the right, a message appearing on many trucks, which probably refers to which side to pass on, but whose true meaning has always escaped me. I fell in love with Indian trucks that day, and looking at them as we drove by always helped distract me from the feeling that I was taking my life in my hands every time I traveled on an Indian road.

The part of the road trip I enjoyed least was the passing. Every car I traveled in while in India spent most of the trip sticking out into traffic beyond the edge of the car or truck in front of it, waiting for a tiny gap in the traffic so that it could pass. The gaps that enticed our drivers were miniscule by my standards, and my heart was in my mouth during the whole maneuver, which involved the obligatory honking and a last-minute, breathtaking swerve back into our lane. I eventually formed the belief that Indian cars (maybe all cars) are endowed with consciousness, and as they pass each other in opposite directions they shrink themselves a little, the way I would pull in my shoulder, to allow another person to pass.

Narrowly escaping death (in my mind, at least), we arrived eventually at the ashram. I'd been told many times, "Oh, you will love it—it's so beautiful," so my expectations were high. But when we got there, I thought the building was strange, with domed towers and arched entrances, but large and gray and streaked with black—not beautiful. The experienced ashramites on the bus said it was too bad the ashram hadn't been painted yet after the recent monsoon rains. I wondered how much difference that could make.

To make matters worse, although Amy and I had been assigned an apartment, when we got there the apartment building turned out to be a construction site. The gray cement walls had dried, but the building was surrounded by a network of bamboo scaffolding tied together with ropes. The framework, which looked like it had been designed on the drawing board of a five-year-old, bore fruit: agile and skinny Indian construction workers who scrambled barefoot up the bamboo like monkeys in a tree. They were aided by a crew of equally skinny and tiny-framed women dressed in saris, their heads adorned with a circular cloth on which they bore large shallow bowls containing loads of bricks or cement, which looked impossibly heavy for their fragile bodies. Thus the work continued, slowly, but did not finish in the five months we were there.

In the next few weeks the ashram was painted soft pastel colors—pink, turquoise, warm pale yellow, early spring green— that brought out the decorative touches in the architecture. But it wasn't until the festival of Diwali, a few weeks after our arrival, that I saw the ashram, and India itself, in its full splendor. One day as I walked out onto the street and looked up at the front of the ashram, the façade sparkled with a web of tiny colored lights that covered the entire surface. Strings of lights had been strung in a pattern of horizontal and vertical panels, and traced the curves of the dome and the arches. Here and there were niches, like medallions, surrounded by a border of lights and inhabited by the images of favorite Indian gods painted in lights that blinked sequentially so that they appeared to move. Ganesh, the elephant-headed god, swung his trunk. Durga, the mother of the universe, rode her tiger, whose legs moved along in blinking lights. Laxmi poured golden coins from her hands. Om flashed on and off. It was beyond magical, beyond fairyland, beyond anything I had expected or thought possible. The effort that had gone into the display was staggering. I stood there drinking it in, transported, and began to see that India had its own beauty.

My favorite manifestation of this beauty, because it occurred over and over, was the garlanding that took place each time there was a ceremony. Ceremonies were a constant event in Indian life, and they all took place against an exquisite backdrop of flower garlands hung from ceiling to floor, abundantly, everywhere. What Americans spend on gadgets and the French spend on food, the Indians spend on beauty, beautiful flowers in particular. The flowers were pink, red, white, yellow. My favorites were the strings of carnations, but there were also garlands of yellow marigolds and champa (frangi-pani) and other flowers I didn't know. It always impressed me that in a poor country like India, nobody seemed to object to lavishing flowers on the temples and meeting places where ceremonies took place. Part of the reason this beauty can be a part of life is that in India there are still people who do hand work. If there were a Walmart in India it would sell perma-nent plastic garlands.

The grounds of the ashram covered many acres, and at the center was a garden with stone paths meandering through it. Throughout the garden were statues of famous saints of India, and beloved gods and mythic heroes. Krishna played his flute there, Tukaram held up his cymbals and chanted, Nandi the bull sat with legs folded under her, and a saint whose name I forget smoked a chillum, right out in the open, to the fascina-tion of most of us. There were cashew trees in the garden, and many papaya and mango trees. There was a bush with heavily perfumed yellow trumpet flowers, which was known to be a potent hallucinogen, and which Baba warned us not to fool with, because it could cause death.

I only heard of one death at the ashram. Across the fields from the compound was a mountain, small but wild looking. Sometimes at night we could see fires on the mountain, and I learned that they were built by hunters who went up there in search of wild animals. Occasionally, adventurous ashramites would climb the mountain, which was thought to possess a sacred vibration. One day a couple of young men went on a climbing expedition. That afternoon there was a bustle in the courtyard, and I heard that one of them had died on the mountain, and a team of ashramites had gone up to get his body and bring it down. The friend who'd been with him de-scribed his death. He said, "He sat down and crossed his legs, went into meditation, and died." It was widely thought that if you were going to die, the ashram was a good place to do it.

At the end of the garden was a cowshed, and near it a deer park. There had once been an elephant, the gift of an Indian devotee, but he was no longer there. The story I heard was that he was wild, and had sometimes thrown his trainer, a strong and fearless young man, against a wall. He was considered untrustworthy, but when Baba came to see him the elephant would reverently garland him with flowers (provided by a human, presumably).

Across the road from the main building were apartments known as the condos, which is where Amy and I lived. It was a small cluster of houses and two-story apartment buildings. On the road between the houses and the ashram were two or three stores. One was fairly grand for a local store. It had two rooms, and stocked the kinds of things Americans in India would want to buy. It had incense and brass statues of deities and clothing and pencils and notebooks and books. It also had a treasure—comic books, Indian comic books in English, of great stories from Hindu scripture and from the great spiritual epic the *Mahabharata*. There we could read about the saint Tukaram, the mystic Mirabai, tales of Krishna as a baby and as a grown-up deity, the exploits of the monkey-god Hanuman and the elephant-headed god Ganesh, and of course the central myth of Hinduism, the sacred text of the *Bhagavad Gita*. We collected them all as avidly as my childhood friends had collected *Superman* comics and *Wonder Woman*. Someday I will read them to my grandchildren.

Near the store was an outdoor café where we could order the sticky-sweet syrupy sodas of India. They served chai too, but most of us preferred to go to the chai shop up the street, where they boiled the buffalo milk in a huge iron pot and the chai tasted heavenly. Across from the chai shop was a tiny bank where we changed our money at the official rate.

Usually, though, we waited for someone to go into Bombay, where it was possible to get a much better rate on the black market. Money-changers were all over Bombay—they often accosted us on the street—but the reliable ones were found in the shops in the huge mall at the Oberoi Hotel, the first-class hotel where most Western businessmen stayed. The Taj was a beautiful and stately hotel, but the Oberoi was modern, had stores, and even a swimming pool. The Taj had a pool too, but it seemed more decorative than functional.

Inside the gates of the ashram was a very different atmosphere from the surrounding area—quiet and peaceful and other-worldly. The entrance consisted of a marble vestibule. At one end was a shelf with a large container of water on it. This was the water fountain of the ashram, and everyone drank from the same pitcher. You had to learn to pour the water into your mouth from a distance of about eight inches above your face. Many people became adept at it, but I never did.

Next to the vestibule was the temple, where there was a statue of Bhagawan Nityananda, and where chants were often held. I once witnessed a remarkable event in the temple. While I was at the ashram, repairs and improvements to the temple were undertaken. In order to accomplish the work, it was considered necessary to remove the living spirit, the spiritual energy called *shakti*, from the Nityananda statue. Brahmin priests were called, and a ceremony was performed during which the *shakti* was removed from the statue and placed in an appropriate vessel for safekeeping. Some months later, when the work was done, everyone at the ashram was invited to attend the ceremony in which the *shakti* was to be put back in the statue. The head Brahmin priest came back, and the ceremony was performed, with incense and the chanting of scriptures and the waving of long ceremonial fans made of ox tails. At the end, the vessel containing the *shakti* was opened, with the Brahmin priest on one side, and Swami Nityananda, who later succeeded Baba, on the other, whispering words into the statue's ears. I could hardly believe what I was witnessing. Without any visible measurable change, the statue transformed from an inanimate object to an enlivened presence. The feeling in the temple was palpably different. The statue was awake. I came away with a new faith in the power of ritual to do what it is intended to do.

Beyond the temple was the marble courtyard, the hub of the ashram. At one end of the courtyard was another, open temple where the morning and evening chants were held. Surrounding the courtyard were dormitories where most of the ashramites lived. Going down the hill out of the courtyard you passed under a trellis grown over with jasmine, whose heavenly perfume made every passage under it a delight. Beyond the jasmine passage was the kitchen of the ashram café whose name—Amrit—means nectar. Past the kitchen was a roofed-over open area with many tables, where they served Western-style food. We spent many pleasant hours there eating breakfast or snacks or an occasional veggie-burger lunch with friends. We became close to many people at the ashram, and all of my trips to Bombay or to Ganeshpuri were in the company of one or some of these friends.

Life at the ashram was simple and quiet. If you haven't experienced it, it is hard to imagine how peaceful it is to live the life of an ashram-dweller. The day is structured around a schedule of sacred chants, some long, some short, some required, some voluntary. They are almost all of a melodiousness and rhythmic power that matches any music I have ever been exposed to. The experience of chanting is uplifting and ecstatic. I remember being told the story of a monastery where the monks spent their days chanting. At one point, an expert was called in to find out how they could do their work more efficiently. He recommended that they stop chanting. Within months, many of the monks were sick. I have come across this story twice, in different settings, and each time it was told as a true story. I don't know. But I believe it.

The day started around six with the chanting of the *Guru Gita*. Most of the ashramites showed up daily for the chant, and the temple and the courtyard were usually filled. The day started off cool enough to require a shawl around your shoulders, but would end up infernally hot. My body had an intense reaction to the heat of India. I can remember lying on my bed at night with a cool breeze flowing over me. My skin was cool, but I felt as though I were burning up inside. The fire inside me never seemed to go out.

After the morning chant we all went to breakfast, where a concoction called sour cereal was served. It was famously good for you, and spicy, and many people found it delicious. I found that I had an intractable mental block about green breakfasts (one ingredient was cilantro), and I could never bring myself to eat it. Instead, I went with a few sybaritic friends to the outdoor café, where coffee and rolls were available.

After breakfast we all went to our jobs, called *seva*—service. Many cooked, some cleaned, and some, like me, worked in the garden. The job I loved best in the New York ashram was working with the video crew, but in India I worked in the garden, repotting plants. I spent the morning potting and watering, and then usually walked around the lovely gardens instead of going to the noon chant. Initially, I started with a different *seva*—painting the statues in the garden, which I enjoyed. But eventually it became too hot for me, and because my heart had been acting up with irregular and rapid heartbeats since I arrived in India, I was given a less demanding job, in the shade.

A friend of mine worked in registration, receiving and organizing visitors to the ashram. Another friend worked on the video crew, taping Baba's trips around the ashram, and the celebrations that took place periodically. There was a large crew of carpenters—the stars of the ashram—who were always busy. There were managers, finance officers, travel arrangers, and a large crew of people who held trays of lentils or grains on their laps and sorted through them, picking out stones. There was a clinic, staffed with a doctor and several nurses; there were plumbers and purchasing agents and a group of swamis who ran the spiritual side of the community.

In the late morning Baba would come out of his house, through a door that opened onto the courtyard, and sit in his long chair and give *darshan*. Anyone who was not otherwise occupied would go to *darshan*—it was the thing we all waited for. Just sitting there and watching Baba and the people who came up to bow to him or touch his feet or talk to him filled the hours with nectar. I never tired of it.

At noon Baba would go inside, and the ashramites would line up in the courtyard to go to lunch. Lunch and dinner were served in the dining room, which was beyond the courtyard and Baba's house. It consisted of a bare floor covered with long strips of plastic, where ashramites sat cross-legged, waiting to be served. In front of each of us was either a stainless steel round tray or, often on holidays, a platter made of three huge leaves sewn together with twine to make a plate. Food at the ashram was simple and healthy and delicious. The servers came around and gave us heaps of rice, vegetable *bhaji*, *chapatis*, and chutney. We ate with our fingers, only ever the right hand because in India the left hand is reserved for a more menial use, and it would shock and offend Indians to see a Westerner eat with the left hand.

Often we were entertained by a member of the ashram video crew, who had been a follower of Maharishi Mahesh

Yogi's Transcendental Meditation movement, and who had reached the stage where he could "fly." He would sit cross-legged at his seat, begin to meditate, and at some point hop, legs still crossed, over his tray into the space between the rows of diners. His friends on the video crew hooted at this demonstration of "flying," but I was impressed.

After lunch it was customary to take a nap. I think almost everyone did—the heat was fierce at that hour. I took refuge in my apartment, where I would nap and take showers. Around three, there was another block of *seva*, and another voluntary chant, which I usually skipped. Sometime in the afternoon Baba came out into the courtyard and gave an afternoon *darshan*. Most people finished *seva* in time to see at least part of the afternoon *darshan*. Often Indian families would bring their children. The mother would put her hand on top of her little child's head and push him into a kneeling position with his forehead touching the floor. They would converse with Baba in Hindi, something I envied acutely. I tried to learn Hindi—I took lessons in New York—but it is a difficult language and it was beyond my skills.

Just before dinner the ashramites gathered to do *arati*, the evening worship chant. After dinner we often had a "fast chant," one in which some of the thousands of names of God are repeated to a hypnotic melody of great beauty—first the men chanting, then the women, in counterpoint, to the accompaniment of drums and cymbals and a harmonium, and guaranteed to transport you to an altered state.

This routine was repeated day after day at the ashram, punctuated by infrequent trips to Bombay and slightly more frequent walks to Ganeshpuri. There was no pressure, no hurrying, no shortage of time, no decisions about what distractions to chase after. I think I could have lived that life forever—if Baba hadn't died and brought it to an end for me.

There was also abundant camaraderie at the ashram. We never discussed it, but we all felt connected by our devotion to the Guru. Even now when we meet, after years of absence, there is an immediate connection, like family.

ॐ

The town of Ganeshpuri was the equivalent of downtown for us. When we had finished our *seva* and we craved a change of scenery, we would walk down the pastoral dirt road, past fields and an occasional cement house surrounded by a cement wall. On the road we would often run into groups of school children dressed in blue and white uniforms—relics of the British rule in India, I suppose. The children would rush up and surround us, calling "What-is-your-name?" We'd repeat our names over and over, ad nauseum. The walk took about twenty minutes and at the end our feet were covered with dust.

Town was a block long. On either side were Indian shops—strictly utilitarian places to buy necessities. On the left was the town restaurant, Ramesh Bhuvan. The front was a half-wall of cement, open at the top, so that you could just see the tops of the heads of diners sitting at the tables inside. The door was an opening in the wall. Inside were about six tables of four chairs each, lined up along both walls in the long narrow space. At one end, near the door, was the kitchen—a few cooking pots and a stove. My friends and I would go there for breakfast, which was pretty much the same as lunch and dinner: rice, vegetables, *chapatis*, or *puris* stuffed with a sweet creamy custard. We would all drink chai.

Near the restaurant was a general store, about six feet wide, with an open counter in the front and a wall of shelves behind the shopkeeper. There you could find things like laundry detergent and salt and cans of food and imitation Kleenex. Across the road was a *bidi*, or cigarette, shop where an Indian man sat cross-legged and rolled cigarettes, which you could buy one at a time. Next to the *bidi* shop was the tailor shop. It was a spacious emporium, quite a bit larger than the other shops, and was run by two brothers. They sold white shirts and pants of exquisite Egyptian cotton, which cost about $1.50 apiece. They would also make you any garment you desired, usually for about the same price. They could copy anything you brought them, and they had a supply of bolts of high-quality cotton, soft and sturdy. They sat at their treadle machines and turned out shirts and skirts and pants for us. The results were unpredictable, but often satisfactory. The worst story I heard was of a pair of shorts they made for my friend Luc, which had a patch pocket on the back center seam, inside.

At the end of the street was the Nityananda Temple, the shrine to Muktananda's guru. It was large and imposing, like a church. It covered the area of a small block, and faced a dusty square. Outside were garland and fruit vendors selling offerings you could bring in and offer to the Nityananda statue. There was also a small ragtag collection of beggars sitting near the temple steps, hoping for alms. This was a common scene outside all Indian temples. At the larger, more important shrines there was sometimes a block-long row of stalls selling offerings and souvenirs, like photos or paintings of the local deity, and bead *malas* (used like rosaries), incense, and *kumkum*, the red powder Indians wear on the third eye.

Closer to the ashram were a few stores that provided services and occasional distraction. The laundry, in particular, was heavily used by everyone. Like the stores in town, it consisted of an open-air cubicle with a counter, behind which were shelves containing piles of folded laundry tied with rough twine. Around the shop and behind it, on the grass and the bare earth, the washed laundry was spread out to dry. Drying was something that took no time at all in India—the clothes were quickly baked in the oven-like heat.

Once you had visited the laundry, they knew you. They took the precaution to write your name in indelible ink inside the waistband or neck of a garment, but they called you by name after the first visit, and to my astonishment, remembered me when I came back after a year's absence. It's just one of the many contrasts that results from the difference between left-brain and right-brain thinking. (Indians think differently from us, which I attribute to relying on different hemispheres.)

The most dramatic and to me, most hilarious example of that difference resides in a story an ashramite told me about someone we both knew. He had gone into Bombay to the post office to make an urgent phone call. Theoretically it was possible to make a phone call from the ashram, because there were phones there, but I had always heard it said that they didn't work. I had no idea what that meant until one day when I tried to call Bombay to make a hotel reservation. The call went through without much delay, and I heard a voice answer at the hotel desk. I couldn't make out what it was saying, but I explained that I wanted to reserve a room. The voice answered, but I didn't have a clue as to what the words were. I repeated my request and heard the same garbled squeaks as the first time. It could have been cacophonous music, or a Martian speaking his native language. The sounds were faint but distinct, but had no relationship to language. At that point, I understood why it was necessary to go to Bombay or write a letter to make your hotel reservations.

So the friend I speak of went to Bombay to make a phone call, and told the person at the telephone desk of the post office that he wanted to make an urgent call to America. The man at the desk told him he'd have to sit down and wait, that the line was very long. He sat and waited and waited and waited for several hours. While he was waiting he noticed that some people came in and got their calls through immediately. Finally he went back to the desk and asked why their calls were going through while he had to wait. The man answered, "You asked to make an urgent phone call. Urgent phone call takes four hours. Ordinary phone call goes right away." (That could have happened in a Paris post office too.)

Once, one of my friends needed to go to the dentist. He was given the name of someone in a town just outside of Bombay. I think in his place I would have flown home, but he was desperate to go because he had a toothache. He asked me to go with him and I said I would, knowing I would not want to go alone if it were me. We left early in the morning, taking a taxi to a nearby town, where there was a train to Bombay. I hadn't thought about what rush hour might be like in India.

When we got to the station it was packed. The train arrived, and it was clearly impossible for it to hold the crowd that waited on the platform. Notwithstanding, we all got in. To my horror, many people clung to the outside of the train, hanging off the windows and doors. Inside we were packed together with barely room to breathe. If you've ever been in the New York subway in rush hour you still have no idea what this was like. Indians have a very different sense of personal space than Westerners. In the ashram, seated in the temple for a chant, it was common for an Indian woman to come in and sit down so close that to me it felt that she was in my lap.

I have noticed this difference in Europe as well. Once, at a movie theater in Paris I was alone because it was the middle of the afternoon. Someone else came in as the movie started and sat down in the empty theater in the seat next to me. And once in Rome I had gone to the railroad station to buy a ticket to Paris. It was early in the morning and the vast station was empty, except for a woman who had entered at the other end and was walking, from a long way off, toward me. I kept walking toward her. When we were close enough to cross paths, she bumped into me.

The Indian train barreled down the track, rocking from side to side. I was afraid it would shake off its outside passengers, but they maintained their hold. At each stop there was a press for the door, and the outside riders got off to let people out of the train, and then hopped back on as it started again. A few stations before ours, we signaled to each other to start toward the door. We wormed our way through the crowd almost to the edge. I didn't want to stand near the open door while the train was moving. I was hoping I could push my way through the one or two people between me and the door when the time came. At our stop we pushed and wormed and called out, and managed at the last second to get off the train. I can still feel the sense of relief that came over me when I was at last on the station platform.

From there we walked a few block to the dentist's office. It was in a small, gray dingy apartment building, up a couple of flights of stairs. I sat in the waiting room while my friend went in. When he came out, pale and shaken, he described to me what had happened. He said he had sat down in the chair and the dentist pulled out a huge pair of pliers. He held out his hands to show me the size—about a foot long. I thought of cartoons I had seen of a dentist pulling teeth with an instrument like that. My friend took one look at the pliers and said, "You're kidding, right?" But no, he wasn't kidding, and the dentist proceeded to pull his tooth out with the cartoon pliers. I took his arm and led him back to the train station, and we went home.

I remember often reflecting on the difference in the

level of physical comfort that Indians expect and what we Westerners are accustomed to. When it was too hot to walk to Ganeshpuri from the ashram, or when we were in a hurry, we would occasionally take a *tonga*—a small, brightly painted carriage with a bench big enough for three, balanced on two large wooden wheels, and topped by a fringed canopy. It was pulled by a horse whose bones poked out under his skin so that he looked like an animated, leather-covered skeleton. The ride cost a few rupees (maybe a quarter) and was a rare luxury. This jolting, bone-cracking, dusty, and smelly ride was the Mercedes of Indian travel, at least in the rural back country where we were living.

The India I knew seemed to be covered with a fine layer of dust. The smell of India is a compound mixture of that dust, automobile exhaust (in the cities), cow dung, smoke from the constant wood fires for cooking and heat, and human waste. It's as much a part of the landscape as the dry fields, the dusty trees, the abundant and fragrant flowers that grow everywhere, and the people and cows who share the streets and sidewalks.

I remember when, back in the U.S., the movie *Gandhi* first came out and we all rushed to see it. At the opening scenes we began to laugh. Where was the dust? Where, for that matter, were the smells, or at least the sources of the smells? It was Hollywood India, not the place we had known.

Nevertheless, there were many exotic pleasures available in India. Amy and I, and later other friends from the ashram, took occasional trips to Bombay, heart in mouth for the whole ride, and started with breakfast at the magnificent Taj Hotel. Everything in the hotel was princely—the huge marble lobby, the façade, the waterfront site, the garden, the rooms, the service. One day, walking out of the hotel, we saw a horse-drawn open carriage pull up to the door. The horse was festooned with garlands and tassels and a harness studded with silver ornaments. In the garlanded open carriage sat a handsome Indian man in a white silk jacket touched with gold embroidery, an impressive white silk turban wound around his head. It was Prince Charming, arriving for his wedding!

There was a little sweet shop tucked into the façade of the hotel. When we ran out of the supply of chocolates we had brought from home, we made it a point to stop at this shop to stock up on candy. They sold honey and spices and other less familiar Indian treats, but the thing we were after was the chocolate bars wrapped in red foil. They were known at the ashram as India's closest approximation to Western candies, and they looked delicious. The first time we bought them, Amy and I unwrapped ours in great anticipation. We took a bite and looked at each other in dismay. It's hard to pinpoint what the difference was. It could have been the addition of some unfamiliar spice that didn't taste sweet to our palates. Or it could have been that it was an imitation of something we knew, and the interpretation missed something in the translation. In any case, the chocolate bars were a horrible disappointment. However, after several months in India, they started to taste delicious to us, and we craved them, and stocked up every chance we got.

Walking down the street from the Taj toward the center of town, we would encounter the reality of the Indian streets. Ragged children begged for rupees. A man without legs, riding on a wheeled platform, rolled up to us and held out his hand. The streets of Bombay were intense. Cars, motorbikes, tongas, bicycles, and cows jammed the roads. Huge bulls strolled through the streets, while the tiny cars and three-wheeled rickshaws maneuvered around them. The smell of exhaust was the only air there was to breathe, and the traffic noise was overpowering. Whole families made camp on the sidewalks and could be seen cooking a meal, washing their hair, living their lives in the public domain.

Once we went to a market street—it was early in my stay in India, and I wanted to see it all. The market specialized in stainless steel kitchenware. There were open-air booths lining both sides of the street, and the wares were set out on tables. As we walked down the center of the street I could feel hundreds of dark eyes fixed on me. There, in that most benign of settings, I suddenly had a full-blown attack of culture shock. I just couldn't handle the numbers of people, the pressure of their gazes, the smells and sounds, the cumulative foreignness of what I was experiencing. I couldn't breathe, and I had to get out of there.

It was the custom at the ashram for the women to dress for ceremonies in saris. That required a trip to Bombay to shop. There is an elaborate ritual to shopping for saris, and it is not watered down for foreigners, because most tourists don't need saris and don't frequent these stores. When you walk in the door of the shop you don't need to say why you are there, because the only thing the shop sells is saris. They are rolled up behind the counter on long tubes, row after row of exquisite silks. As you walk in the owner greets you like a guest in his home. He invites you to a large open space at the end of the shop, or upstairs to his showroom, an empty floor with cushions on it. As you sit he asks what you would like to drink. "Tea? Cold soda?" We always agreed to cold soda, because in India it is always hot. He calls an assistant and sends him out for soda. Another assistant brings in an armful of tubes of silk and places them at the feet of the shop owner. You look over the rolls and point to your favorites. The owner grabs one and with a huge arm gesture he unfurls it across the floor. Saris are made of six yards of silk, and the effect is like a river of silk at your feet. They are all breathtaking—you can't resist a gasp as they unroll before your eyes. On almost every sari there is a print that runs down the center, a border at both edges, and a yard or so of a horizontal design at the end that sums up the motifs of the border and creates a decorative tail that hangs down your back when the sari is worn. Never losing patience, the shop owner unrolls stream after stream of silk. Some are trimmed in gold thread. Some are woven so that if you look at them one way they are one color, and another color the other way. You drink your sticky-sweet soda and try to decide which of these rivers of silk is right for you. Once you have chosen, the assistant swiftly and dexterously folds it and folds it and folds it into a manageable shape. This is a profession in itself. I have never been able to fold a sari without someone to help me, and it takes me at least four times as long.

That was something I loved doing, but my all-time favorite shopping in Bombay was in a little market street behind a famous temple. On that street they sold perfumed oils, which is what I went there for. They also sold tiny decorations that were meant to adorn your household gods. There were tiny crowns an inch long to put on the god's head, strings of tiny beads for bracelets, little necklaces of chain or cut glass. There were also almond-shaped eyes of various sizes, in case you wanted to make your own *murti* (an image of a god). This is, in fact, a common practice in India, where I have often encountered trees or rocks with a bump on them suggestive of an elephant's head and trunk, that have been painted, garlanded, and worshiped with *kumkum* powder on the third-eye spot and garlands at their feet.

The striking lesson I learned from India was the daily and universal presence of the sacred. Every town had its shrines, which were actively frequented. Pictures of deities and saints were hung in every store. Automobiles and trucks always had a picture of a deity or a guru, and appropriate decorations—a shrine on the dashboard, a garland around a picture. Indian people are named after gods or saints or sacred qualities, such as *Ananda*—bliss. Almost all Indians wear *kumkum* on their foreheads to symbolize the existence of the third eye, the eye of intuition, the eye that sees spirit. The Indian greeting is "*Namaste*," said with hands folded—"I bow to the spirit in you." The pervasiveness of the sacred in everyday street life gradually takes hold of you, and when it's not there anymore, as in America, you wonder why.

❧ SIXTEEN
The Bugs of India

I REMEMBER STANDING AT THE ashram bulletin board watching an insect make its way up the board from bottom to top. It had a narrow body and large, translucent green wings and long skinny legs with claws at the ends like tiny crab pincers. It clung to the cork surface with its tiny claws and worked its way up slowly, one leg after the other, like climbing a mountain. I couldn't take my eyes off it, because it was the biggest bug I'd ever seen. It might have been six or seven inches long, and to my mind it surpassed the category of insect and entered into some other class of being by virtue of its size. I thought of it as a person, entitled to personhood because of the amount of space it occupied. I left before it got to the top—I didn't want to be around when it started flying.

I never ever walked barefoot in India, because I was unwilling to have a close encounter with some of the things you could find crawling on the ground. The one I most feared, though it was harmless, was a black shiny beetle about four inches long. As it walked its head swung loosely from side to side like an elephant's. It did not seem possible to me to put this creature in the same category as an ant or a ladybug. It

wasn't just size—these beings had a weightiness that commanded consideration. They were not just bugs underfoot that you
never give a thought to as you squash, or don't squash, them. I
had always been afraid of bugs, and tried to keep them out of
my mind. But these creatures did not let you overlook them.

Another inhabitant you wanted to stay away from was a
tiny snake that I never saw, but others at the ashram did. It
was about three inches long and was called a five-stepper. The
story was that once it bit you, you could take five more steps,
and then you were dead. I never heard of anyone at the ashram being bitten by one, but I did hear that the brother of a
friend woke up from a nap and found one on his night table.
They were reputed to swim around in the flooded fields that
surrounded the ashram. The fields were usually bone dry, but
during monsoon they became vast shallow lakes that covered
the area between the ashram and the town of Ganeshpuri.
People often cut across the fields to go to town, but during the
monsoon the shortcut became hazardous.

There were other health hazards in India that I'd been
warned about but didn't encounter. I'd been told that cuts
got infected easily, and you had to treat them at once to avoid
problems. I never got a cut while I was there, but I did hear of
people who got local infections that persisted for months. The
other universal warning was about amoebas. Don't drink the
water, don't eat raw vegetables—standard tourist advice. We
took it, brushing our teeth with bottled water and avoiding sal-
ads on our trips to Bombay hotels and restaurants. Everyone
was careful, but when we all got home and got tested, everyone I knew who had been there had amoebas in their system.

We all took vitamins in an effort to keep ourselves healthy.
One day there was a problem with the sewer system, and the
ashram crew had to open it up to clear it out. It turned out
to be clogged with a huge clot of vitamin pills, all more or

less intact. Since then I've never had the same confidence in vitamin supplements that I had before.

The one thing I was not careful about was the *prasad* they handed out in the temples. (*Prasad* is a gift, usually food, from a great being or saint.) Visiting temples is something you do in India, the way one visits the museums in Europe. We went there for the blessings, but also to see the temples. They often had marvelous, colorfully painted statues of deities, wrapped in rich silk shawls trimmed in gold and garlanded with long ropes of flowers. Of course we regularly visited the temples in Ganeshpuri, most of which were dedicated to Nityananda, Baba's guru. We also went frequently to temples in Bombay, and the few times I traveled to other towns I always called on the local deity. At the end of whatever form of worship was being performed, sometimes just the presentation of a garland I'd bought outside, and sometimes a ceremonial worship called *puja*, we would file up to the local priest, who would hand out *prasad*. Always there was holy water, which I would cup in my hands and sip, and then rub on the top of my head where the crown chakra is and on my forehead and throat (two more upper chakras). I did this because everyone else did. If there was *prasad* in the form of food, I ate it. I decided from the beginning that it was a holy substance and I would take my chances with it. Who knows? Maybe my amoebas came from the prasad. It was worth it.

My heart problems—arrhythmia, tachycardia, preventricular contractions—started in India. Whether India caused them I cannot know. I am suspicious, though, because they started almost immediately after I got there. The heart is the location of a major chakra, and I have always considered that my heart's behavior has something to do with the amount of spiritual energy flowing through it, beginning with my arrival in India. It may be more energy than I can easily accommodate, or it may speak of the difficulty the physical form has in trying to contain the fullness of vibrational experience that lies beyond the physical world.

I got rid of the amoebas. If I could get rid of the heart symptoms I would, but I don't seem to be able to, so I live with them. India gave me many gifts. This is just one of them. I won't turn it down.

☙ SEVENTEEN

Passage of Power

WE RETURNED TO INDIA IN May of 1982, for a celebration of Baba's birthday. Our return was a homecoming this time. The ashram was still decked out in its pastel coats of paint, the *dhobi* (laundry man) knew my name, I had brought with me items from a list I had created myself, and the apartment we'd been promised for the previous visit was at last ready to be occupied. We were surprised and delighted.

In the interval between visits we had heard that Malti, Swami Nityananda's sister, was to be given *sannyas* in May and was named Baba's co-successor, along with her brother. Baba announced that the celebration of his birthday would be the occasion of the passage of power from him to his two successors. This was to be a huge occasion, and all his Indian and Western devotees who could make it were planning to attend.

Amy and I arrived some days before the big event. We took a taxi from the Bombay airport, dropped our trunks in the reception area, and rushed to the courtyard to greet Baba. He was sitting in his long chair, alone except for his attendant, Noni. Amy and I went up to him and bowed before him. He greeted us warmly and told us that he was about to go to the cowshed where Malti's *sannyas* ceremony was taking place. To our great astonishment and joy, he asked us if we would like to come along. He got up and started away—it was as though he'd been waiting for us to arrive. We asked Noni, "Did Baba say we should come with him now?" We were unable to believe that it had really happened. Noni answered, "Yes, I think so," giving us a strange look as though he couldn't believe it either. We followed them to the cowshed, expecting to be barred at the door, but no one stopped us, and we went in.

The cowshed was a long, low white adobe building with half walls and a thatched roof supported by columns. There were no cows in it today. The air inside was thick with smoke and the sound of Brahmin priests chanting. Malti sat on the floor in front of a small fire, dressed in white robes, her head shaved, her eyes lowered. She was following the instructions given to her by Bhau Shastri, the head Brahmin. Every so often in the ceremony she was instructed to offer flowers or rice to the fire, or to dip leaves in a vessel of water and sprinkle the water around. Her long, graceful fingers executed the rituals as Bhau Shastri instructed. The ritual, the chanting, and the smoke were hypnotic, and we stood and stared, rapt and ecstatic at being able to witness this event. At one point Baba stood up from his position next to Malti, and drawing a blackened twig from the fire, struck it across her cheek, leaving a long narrow black trace. I had no idea why he'd done it, but the moment was charged with an unforgettable electric energy.

I looked around at the few people assembled there. Three or four of the women swamis were seated in a corner behind Malti. Three Brahmin priests chanted around the fire. The video crew, consisting of a director and a cameraman, were next to us, taping the ceremony. Baba and Malti sat before us on the floor. And Amy and I and one other woman stood near the entrance to the cowshed, watching it all.

After about half an hour Bhau Shastri suddenly caught sight of us. He jumped up and began yelling at Baba and waving his arms excitedly, pointing at us. We got the drift, but someone explained to us later that women were not allowed to attend a *sannyas* ceremony unless they were swamis—it was forbidden by custom or scripture and was believed to make them sterile. (This was not a concern for the swamis, who were celibate.) As Bhau Shastri yelled and gesticulated, Baba began to laugh. He laughed heartily throughout the noisy protest, but finally he signaled to Noni that we should leave. We filed out the doorway. A short way up the hill was a crowd of ashramites who had gathered to observe what they could manage to see from a respectful distance outside the cowshed. When they saw us come out they stared in disbelief. I have never before or since been the object of such envious gazes as they sent our way that day.

Malti was given the name Chidvilasananda, which means "the bliss of the play of consciousness." Baba's autobiography was called *Play of Consciousness*, so Malti, like her brother, had been singled out with a special name—an honor, but a mouthful.

The ceremony of the Passage of Power was set for Baba's birthday, the first full moon in May. On the morning of the occasion, Amy and I dressed in saris, took our seat cushions and meditation mats, and went down to the *mandap*, the roofed-over open-air shed where all *yagnas* took place. Again, to my great joy and gratitude, we were given seats in the front row, very near the fire pit. We sat and watched as the crowd poured in. The *mandap* was full to overflowing, and many people were seated outside, sitting on walls or standing to be able to see. After a while there was the familiar buzz, and Baba walked in, dressed in orange silk and followed by Swami Nityananda and Swami Chidvilasananda. They were dressed in orange silk too, their heads shaved and bowed. They were both wearing *malas* (ropes of prayer beads) made of rudraksha beads, the brown seeds of the rudraksha tree that bear naturally occurring designs on them, grooves that circle the bead and look like secret messages. The beads are highly revered in India and are the preferred material for prayer beads. These *rudraksha* beads were the largest I had ever seen, about the size of marbles, and each bead was capped on both sides with gold. The *malas* were spectacular and drew all our gazes. I was told they were a special gift from Baba.

After the ceremonious march in, the festivities began with the usual rituals of the chanting of the Brahmin priests and lighting the fire with the fire sticks. The ceremony had not proceeded very far when there was a sudden drenching downpour of rain. It was raining buckets. The crowd went wild, even those sitting outside, who were soaked to the skin. Everyone was cheering and screaming and applauding and shouting, *"Sadgurunath Maharaj Ki Jay!"* ("Praise to the Guru," a phrase that began and ended just about every significant event at the ashram.) It's important to understand the context: it rains in India only in the rainy season. It does not rain in the dry season. They don't have climate in the sense that we do; they have categories, and nature defines and also obeys the categories, with appropriate behavior. In addition, rain is considered the most auspicious weather phenomenon, and an occasion that is blessed with rain is truly blessed.

The ceremony proceeded in high spirits. At the appropriate time, the two new swamis sat on the ground before Baba, and he sat on the ground facing them and performed various rituals similar to the ones we'd seen in the cowshed. He poured flower petals over the heads of the two disciples, sprinkled them with water from the jars in front of them, and whispered in their ears. At one point a silver bowl filled with water was brought and someone washed Baba's feet ceremonially. A guru's feet are considered to be a potent outlet for his spiritual energy, and his feet are worshiped with appropriate chants ("Hymn to the Feet of the Guru") and the water in which they are bathed is considered holy. Some of the water in the bowl was poured into a white conch shell and during the ceremony Baba poured that water over the heads of the two swamis before him.

After the rituals were completed, the two stood up and went to the fire pit, where they poured ghee into the fire, accompanied by the droning, compelling chanting of the priests. As they poured, the fire leaped up and licked the edges of the pit and poured forth clouds of black smoke that curled around the room. Then the ceremony was over, and we walked around the fire 108 times, the ritually prescribed number, soaking up all the *shakti* (spiritual energy) that was bouncing around the room. My love of walking around the fire pit kept me in the *mandap* after most people had left. Amy stayed too, and we saw several swamis starting to clean up. We went to the edge of the central platform to watch, and the swami who was in the center picked up the white shell and brought it over to where we stood. As we stood there, he poured the water over Amy's head and mine. I think a king who is anointed could not feel more honored than I felt in that moment.

ଌ

I stayed in India for a month that time, and then went home. Baba came back to the ashram in New York for the summer, and we spent the time in our usual pursuits, going to the ashram for the evening programs, chanting, and seeing our ashram friends. At the end of the summer Baba went back to India and we stayed home. I wasn't sure when I would return to India.

One day in October a friend from the ashram invited us to take a plane ride with him. He was a licensed pilot but hadn't yet qualified at the local airport, so he was required to demonstrate his competence with the plane we wanted to rent. He invited us to go up with him for the test. He and the instructor sat in the front of the tiny plane, and Amy and I sat crammed in the back. He did a few touch-and-goes, landing and taking off in one smooth swoop, and then the instructor told him to cut the engine. I was not prepared for this, but it was too late for second thoughts. Our friend did as he was told, and the plane went silent. It was a heart-stopping moment. We floated noiselessly above the earth for a few minutes, and then he switched on the engine and I breathed again.

We flew around for a while, over our house and over the ashram and the hills, studded with trees turning red and gold, and then we landed and went home. As we walked in the door the phone rang. It was a friend from the ashram. He told me to get Amy on the phone too, and then he told us that Baba had left his body.

We never spoke about Baba dying. It was considered that his body had died, but he was still with us. We said he had taken *mahasamadhi*. (*Samadhi* is the blissful state of consciousness available to meditators and other fortunate beings who attain it spontaneously. *Maha* means great.) There is a story about Sri Ramana Maharshi, one of the great saints of India. He was very sick, and his disciples were gathered around him. One of them begged him not to leave them. "Where would I go?" was his answer.

The thought that Baba was still with us was little comfort in that moment. Amy and I were speechless. We were silent for so long that our friend said, "Guys—I have to go now. I

have things to do." He was one of the managers of the ashram, and there were many things for him to do. We hung up.
I was still unable to talk, or even to think. The meaning of my
life had changed in a second, and I felt totally adrift. Baba,
so firmly planted in my heart and my life, was gone. I should
surely have been aware of the possibility of that happening,
but it had never once entered my mind. Baba had become my
life, and I guess I thought of my life as eternal through him.

The hubbub had already started at the ashram. Plane reservations were being made for the "important" people, and
particularly for the video crew. I had no thought of going to
India. What for? Baba was already gone. All I could do now
was witness the funeral, and I had no taste for that. A day
went by, and then suddenly, without thinking, I knew that I
was going. I hurried to call the ashram to make plane reservations for Amy and me. At that point the direct flights were
all booked, and we were given a flight that involved changing planes somewhere in Europe, which would therefore take
much longer to get to India. When I told Luc, one of my
dearest ashram friends and a member of the video crew (and
in possession of a reservation on a direct flight), he said, "You
won't make it. You will get there too late."

The entire lengthy trip to India was riddled with anxiety
for me, as I fretted about Luc's words and worried frantically
that we would arrive too late. I tried mentally to hurry the
plane or make the time pass faster—useless exercises that demonstrated and exacerbated my anxious state. When we arrived
in Bombay I was desperate. We jumped in a taxi and drove
to Ganeshpuri, a drive that did nothing to soothe my state.
When we got to the outskirts of town, at the place where cars
turn off the main road to drive to the ashram, the road was
so jammed with people that the taxi could not proceed. We
grabbed our suitcases (we had packed lightly this time) and

ran down the half mile of road to the ashram. At the gates was a crowd of Indians about nine deep, standing in a semi-circle and barring our way. A crowd of Indians is pretty much impenetrable, a solid object. My heart sank. We rushed forward, to the edge of the crowd. As we got close the crowd saw us, and parted. It was like the Red Sea opening. People stood aside and we went through. I felt washed over by the caring the gesture implied. We entered the ashram, dropped our bags, and rushed to Baba's house, where devotees were filing through to view his body, garlanded and seated in lotus posture. When I saw him I started crying, and I pretty much didn't stop for a month. We left Baba's room and went out into the courtyard. It was packed with devotees, all crying. People came up to us and hugged us. The atmosphere was astonishing. You could feel the love in the air, palpable. What had once been a group of seekers, some friends, some foes, with the usual issues and differences common to groups, had coalesced into a community, united in our grief.

Only half an hour after we arrived, Baba's body was placed in an open truck to be driven slowly down the dusty road to Ganeshpuri, where he would be taken to the Nityananda Temple for his final *darshan* with his guru. Amy and I joined the crowd to follow the truck. The road was packed solid with devotees, and the truck moved at a funereal pace. Voices chanted and finger cymbals tinkled and drums banged. The dust of the road rose and mingled with the cloud of love and grief that followed the truck.

There was no way to squeeze into the packed temple, so we went back to the ashram. A chant had been started in the courtyard temple as soon as the news of Baba's death had come out. The chant was *"Om Namo Bhagavate Muktanandaya,"* which means roughly, "I bow to the Guru Muktananda." It was particularly poignant because it had always been sung

"*Om Namo Bhagavate Nityanandaya*" (Baba's guru) while Baba was alive. The change of syllable brought home with terrible impact the reality that Baba was gone.

The chant went on day and night, every day for a month. No matter what the hour, there were always people chanting, and a drummer and cymbals and a harmonium player. The chant became the air we breathed, soaked into our pores and surrounded us. It was slow and mournful and beautiful, and as soon as I sat down to chant, my tears would start again. I bought the tape of that chant, thinking I would play it at home, but it was about four years before I could hear it without crying.

Although I had heard over and over, and believed, that when the guru leaves his body his larger and more real form is still there, I found I couldn't get over feeling desolate at the loss of Baba's form. I had taken such delight in his presence and in the life that went on around him, which had become my life. I was unwilling to let go of my attachment to his physical presence, even though I had no choice. I stayed stuck in mourning him for more than a year, inconsolable. I longed for dreams of him, and they came, but not often enough.

The one comfort I had was that his *shakti* had been passed on to his two young successors. Bereft though I was, I took some comfort in imagining that the life of the ashram could continue around them. The first summer after Baba's *mahasamadhi* they came to the ashram in New York, and the old way of life was, for a time, restored. It soon became apparent, though, that the ashram had split into two camps. The two young successors sat on the platform at the front of the meditation hall during evening programs, and at the end of the program the *darshan* line formed. There were now two *darshan* lines, however. Not only were there his and hers lines, but it developed over the course of the summer that you had to choose which *darshan* line to go on and stick with it. I had been switching back and forth between them every evening, but then I heard through the very active grapevine that that was unacceptable. You had to show your loyalty to Chidvilasananda by choosing her *darshan* line every night. I was having none of it, and I continued to frequent both lines, but if you lived in the ashram and wanted to be part of the inner circle that was not a choice.

Both these young successors had great attractions for Baba's devotees. You cannot receive the *shakti* of a great guru and remain an ordinary person. Swami Nityananda had a lovely, sweet, and humble presence and a profound devotion to the Guru that was evident. Swami Chidvilasananda was exquisitely beautiful, perhaps even more so with her head shaved, and had a captivating smile. She exuded an air of fervent spirituality. Both of them took power from what had been their close relationships with Baba. Chidvilas, as we called her (and who later became Gurumayi) seemed to relish her power and enjoy wielding it. Nityananda did not.

The summer wore on with the ashram becoming more and more polarized. It was a distressing time. When fall came the two new gurus went back to India. Amy went with them and I did not. Amy was newly married. Chidvilas had performed the ceremony in an Indian-style wedding at our house, complete with saris, garlands, and a huge crowd of ashramites invited at the last minute by Chidvilas as she left the ashram to come to the wedding. Amy had married Neela, one of the ashram carpenters, the elite crew of the ashram. Now he had been requested by Nityananda to come to India to construct appropriate living quarters for the new Guru. They went off for six months, and I stayed home, continuing to go to the ashram for the chants and ceremonies and for the evening programs, which were conducted by swamis.

CR

During the last year of Baba's stay in the Catskills, rumors began circulating that Baba was having sexual relationships with young girls from the ashram. It blew into a major scandal, and several people who had been close to Baba left. I thought the whole thing was absurd. I knew Baba to be a great being, and I could not imagine that sexual appetite would tempt him to be less than he was. Others were extremely upset, but I was not. It was not until the winter after Baba died that I heard from close friends that a close friend of theirs had confided that her daughter was one of the girls. I tried to resist this knowledge, but I couldn't. I had to accept that the story must be true. It blew me out of the water. I went into one of the deepest depressions of my life. I was alone in the house all weekend, and I wrestled with the devil. "I've been wasting my life on a false guru." "None of his teachings are true." "It was all a lie." "He is not a guru." "There is no God." "I have been a fool." Negative thoughts assailed me, devastating me. I felt betrayed and humiliated, and despaired of ever believing spiritual teachings again.

This went on for two days and a night. At the end of the day on Sunday I suddenly pulled into calm waters. I began to notice that through all the tirades, I could not stop loving Baba. I could not get him out of my heart. I decided that my mind would never be able to resolve the paradox, and I would stop trying. I came to rest in a place where my love for and faith in Baba were intact, and I had an inexplicable event to integrate. The best I could do was to tell myself, "That didn't happen in my world." I remembered my image of the Guru as a mirrored globe, like the ones you see in dance halls, revolving and reflecting. The Guru, I thought, reflects everyone as they are, all different. In my little square of mirror, Baba had not taken part in that story. My concept of the Guru had gone beyond the physical existence, and that is where I remain.

I have observed that many of the gurus I've been aware of have given their disciples similar paradoxes to resolve. Do they abscond with money? Have sexual relations with their devotees? Drink to excess? What are they telling us?

The guru can take you far on the spiritual path. Simply being in the presence of a great being can raise your vibrations and change your life. Given a choice, I would have stayed in that rapturous womb forever. Who would want to leave? Baba's *mahasamadhi* was the first expulsion from the Garden, and my terrible weekend of doubt was the second. I conclude that we must all climb the final peak on our own. No one can carry you up the mountain. The guru is the reflection of your own self, and at the end you come to recognize that you are one, not two. The outer guru has led you to the discovery of the inner guru, the divine being that dwells in us all.

♋ EIGHTEEN
Putsch

THERE IS A BELIEF IN India that when the guru leaves his body
he stays with his disciples for the next three years. After that
time, on the anniversary of his *mahasamadhi*, all his particles
leave the earth. To honor the occasion for Baba, a major ceremony was planned in India for October 1985, and I planned
to go. The two young gurus would be there, and thousands of
devotees from around the world were expected. I was delighted to have the use of our apartment, because it was turning
out to be difficult to find a room at the ashram for that time.

The ceremony took place a few days after I arrived. It took
the form of the installation of the two successors into their
new roles. They sat side by side in the *mandap*, garlanded and
shawled, and received the long line of devotees who had come
to be with them. Nityananda, who was usually the mellow-
est of presences, looked strange and intense. His eyes were
glittery and his face had a fierce look that was utterly unlike
him. After the ceremony, people started to talk about his appearance. That turned out to be the least of it. That night
during the chant he failed to show up to do his usual drumming. The drumbeat drives and energizes the chant, and the

chants where Nityananda was the drummer were noticeably more powerful. It was almost unheard of for him not to be at the chant.

The next day rumors started flying around the ashram. It was said that Nityananda was being held in his apartment by Chidvilas's followers. We heard that he had been beaten and drugged, and that his *mala* from Baba had been taken away. His own followers were not allowed to see him, with rare exceptions. We were told that he was being accused of being insufficiently spiritual: of having sexual relationships with girls (including swamis); of spending a night at a casino in Las Vegas on his way to the West Coast. We were told that Chidvilas had announced that Nityananda had been appointed by Baba only to help her for her first three years as Guru, and now his successorship was finished. I also heard that two of his closest devotees had been beaten, and that Indian devotees had been herded into the meditation chamber in the cellar and threatened. The atmosphere of the ashram had become unbelievably intense. It felt like a war. This most peaceful of places had been turned into a battleground. It was unbearable to me, and I left.

I knew that some of the things Nityananda had been accused of were true, but that seemed irrelevant to me. There was no excuse for the degradation of the sacred space of the ashram that I had witnessed. With immense sorrow I realized that the ashram was finished for me. I knew it could never be the same, though I had no idea what form it would take. When I got home I had no intention of going back to the ashram. It would leave a huge hole in my life, almost as big a hole as the loss of Baba had left me with.

After a week or two at home in New York, I received an invitation to come to a special evening program. Curious to know what would happen, I went. It turned out to be a panel of swamis. They were seated in a row in the front of the meditation hall, and they were taking turns speaking. First, one gentle and soft-spoken swami related how she had had sexual relations with Swami Nityananda. Then another spoke and another, telling stories of his profligate ways. It soon became a feeding frenzy, with orange-clad swamis, their heads shaved to show their dedication and to let the inner light shine forth, interrupting each other and saying, "Now it's my turn," falling all over each other to tell lurid stories. I could hardly believe what I was witnessing. This was the sacred meditation hall where we had gathered to be in Baba's presence and to chant God's name together. They were desecrating the temple, and it closed forever any lingering yearning I had to continue to be part of the ashram.

Later I heard that Nityananda had been taken to Hawaii as a prisoner when Chidvilas went there on her tour of ashrams. I'd heard that a friend had managed to get a message to him, and had arranged to help him escape through a window of his room to a waiting car, where his close followers took him away and brought him back to the U.S. He was in California, recovering.

That summer Chidvilas came back to New York. She now ran the ashram. Amy and I were informed that we were not allowed in the ashram. It wasn't what we had done, but what we had not done. We had not demonstrated our loyalty to Chidvilasananda.

In the next few years Nityananda came back to the East Coast, where a group of loyal Indian devotees helped him establish an ashram in a house in New Jersey. He began to hold programs. It was said that they were often interrupted by a crew of Chidvilas's followers, who stood outside the door and took down the names of the people who went in, or threw skunk oil into the room where devotees had gathered or, once, beat up one of Nityananda's Indian followers. All this was fascinating, like a soap opera, but not like a spiritual path. I gave up hope of having a guru again, and turned inward to put into practice what I had learned from Baba.

I don't know how much of what I heard is true. Many gurus have had rumors floating around them. I did not attempt to learn the truth. The guru gives his or her followers a conundrum which they must work out for themselves. It was apparent to me that Chidvilasananda was not my guru, and later it became evident that Nityananda was not as well. Those things are for someone else to deal with.

CR NINETEEN
My Dance with Cancer Continues

FOR FIFTEEN YEARS I HAD had a lump in my breast. Every doctor who ever looked at it said, "It's nothing to worry about. This kind never becomes malignant." So when it started to get bigger I didn't worry about it. That went on for about two years until, after talking to a friend about it, she said I'd better get it looked at right away. Then I began to worry. I had to hunt for the surgeon who had removed the last lump—he had moved his office and had stopped sending me checkup notices—and I went to New York to see him. When we parked the car and I went to put money in the meter, I saw that someone had written on that meter "God loves you."

The surgeon knew immediately that it was malignant. He was furious at me. He yelled at me for not coming in for checkups, and he acted like I was dead already. He told me, "Women who have this kind of recurrence usually have cancer all over their bodies." (Was this to punish me?) It was like a death sentence. Years later I put the picture together and realized that he was one of the doctors who had looked at the lump and said, "This kind never gets malignant."

He removed the lump in his office under local anesthesia,

told me that he would give me the name of someone to see next (which he never did), and I went home in a state of panic—the first and only time that breast cancer has frightened me. Not that I thought it was a picnic, but before, I could handle it. This time I was paralyzed with fear. When I got home I curled up on the couch in a fetal position and stayed there. It was a few weeks before I came out of my paralysis. I had gotten a clear message that I was now dead. It wasn't cancer that frightened me. It was my doctor. He had scared me silly, and I became a basket case.

Amy took over and cared for me. I just lay on the couch. I took Rescue Remedy, my Bach Flower guardian angel, every three minutes all day long. Eventually, slowly, I began to surface from my terror enough to read the book I had bought when we stopped for lunch at a health food store on the way home from the doctor. The book was called *The Secret of Healing*, and the message can be summed up in one sentence: don't think about the problem; think about God. I felt like a drowning person who happens upon a log. I clutched onto that message as I clutched the bottle of Rescue Remedy, and I rode through the storm with the help of both. The advice the book gave was one of those messages that come into your life and change everything. It made total sense to me, and I did it. I banished worry from my mind and thought about God. I did it without expectation of what effect it would have. I did it the way you put one foot in front of the other when you walk, without questioning why or how.

I surfaced a little more and made a plan. I decided I'd go on a macrobiotic diet. Amy made me an appointment to see Michio Kushi—we were lucky; it wasn't easy to get an appointment with him. We went to Boston for a weekend of learning about macrobiotics and how to cook the food. The weekend was informative and inspiring. Kushi had the aura of a master.

He told me what to eat and what not to eat, and he told me to sing. "Sing in the car," he said. "While you're driving. Loud."

We went home and threw away all the food in the pantry. We went to our health food store, the one where I'd bought the healing book, and bought all the strange foods and sea vegetables and equipment of a macrobiotic diet, and went home and started a new way of life. The diet was time-consuming and effortful. Amy did it all—I was still debilitated from the terror the doctor had plunged me into. Amy joined me on the diet, and we dedicated ourselves to a strange and healthy way of eating. The best thing about it was the number of unhealthy or controversial foods it eliminated from our lives. I stopped eating sugar, flour, packaged food, potatoes, tomatoes, raw food. All that was okay, and I felt supported and healthier and kind of noble. There were two major drawbacks we had to deal with, though. For one thing, the diet separated us from our friends, who stopped coming to our house for meals, and whose cooking we could no longer eat.

That was bad, but there was something worse, and it eventually drove me off the macrobiotic diet. I was forbidden to eat fruit. I was on the so-called healing diet, which was more restricted than the standard diet, and fruit was considered too yin for me. I stood it for as long as I could—about five months—and then one day I heard myself thinking, "I would kill for an apple." I went out and bought myself apples and ate one, and I added apples to my diet, but that was the beginning of the end of macrobiotics for me. I realized that my body had gotten healthier but my mind had gotten into a severely contracted state, and I didn't think it was good for me. Little by little I widened my diet, until it was *my* diet, not the macrobiotic diet. I kept some things—a preference for whole foods was the best. And I didn't eat sugar for years. It began to taste slightly obscene to me—like a mistake.

Cancer is an enormous challenge, as anyone who's had it knows. You are faced with so many emotions—yours and others'—and tough decisions to make at a time when you feel that your life is on the line and your family and friends are freaking out. The search for the right doctor is the first hurdle, and if you're successful you find that the next one is deciding what your healing path is. If you're lucky, your doctor will help you decide. Many doctors feel that they know and you don't, and many are under the illusion that you don't want to know—you want them to tell you. Everyone has advice for you, and finding your way through all the voices to your own voice is like cutting your way through jungle undergrowth. Again, if you are lucky your family and friends will support your choices and even be helpful about getting information and sorting through it all. Complicating all this is the fear that most people experience, and the fear their loved ones feel, and everyone's desire to protect the others. One thing I learned is that everyone's healing path is different. Each one's path fits them, fits their lives and their life lessons and who they are and who they are becoming.

In my search for the right doctor I went to see one who turned out to have nothing to offer me himself, but who told me about Bernie Siegel. I bought his book on the way home, and after reading it I wrote to him. I said I was tired of being scared to death by doctors and asked if he'd see me. He wrote me back a handwritten note and told me to call for an appointment. When I got to his office in Connecticut, I knew everything was going to be different there. He was "Bernie," not "Dr. Siegel," and he acted like a human being—a big human being, but still, a human.

He had me draw some pictures, he asked me questions and listened to the answers, and then he asked me what the gain was from having cancer.

I answered, "It has reestablished the closeness with my daughter that we had when she was a child."

He said, "Well, maybe that's it."

A torrent of tears poured from my eyes, as if I were an iceberg that was suddenly and definitively melting. I felt as though Bernie had reached inside me and opened me up, like those psychic surgeons from the Philippines you see on television, reaching bloodlessly inside a patient's skin and pulling out stuff. Bernie agreed to be my doctor, and I went home feeling I was in good hands.

He suggested I take tamoxifen. Despite my suspicion of all things pharmaceutical, I agreed to follow his advice. I took the pills and did numerous drawings and visualizations featuring the pills in various healing scenarios. The need to surround the drug with suggestions of healing properties should perhaps have raised a flag—and maybe it did, but I ignored it. After being on tamoxifen for about five months, I had a significant dream. I had been having fairly frequent dreams with otherworldly healing personages in them, giving me advice. Sometimes I could remember or understand what they said, and sometimes not. In this dream a wise-person figure appeared to me and told me I was taking something toxic. He tried to tell me what it was, and tried to spell it: occisomething. I woke up knowing exactly what he meant. I went off the tamoxifen the next day.

Amy's husband—she was married to an ashramite then— brought to my attention the Kelley Program for cancer. I'd heard about it years ago, from a woman at the ashram who had survived cervical cancer. I decided that if I ever felt I was in bad trouble I would go on the Program. But for now I didn't feel I needed it. I was fine, the surgery and the macrobiotic diet seemed to have worked for me, and I continued with my practice of thinking about God when my worries came back. I was relieved and happy to have survived so many rounds with my demanding dance partner, and immensely grateful to the English surgeon who had spared me the horrors of chemotherapy. I wrote another poem about death, this one peaceful and accepting.

Death plays his silent flute to me
And dances on the grassy hill in front of my house
His skin glows blue, his eyes beckon
Not yet, I say
There are things I haven't finished
He laughs a sweet laugh and his feet stamp in the grass
Come whenever you want, he says
And keeps dancing

STRANGE HAPPENINGS

I WAS IN AMY'S KITCHEN *in Vermont, washing dishes while she put baby Benjamin to bed. I was singing the song from* Carousel: *"What's the use of wond'rin if he's good or if he's bad? He's your feller and you love him, that's all there is to that." As I sang I was thinking of Nick, Amy's partner. Amy and her carpenter husband, Neela, had divorced after a few years. There were incompatibilities, but the main reason seemed to be the division caused by Chidvilas— Neela continued to go to the ashram and Amy didn't. After that, Amy entered into a stormy relationship with Nick, whom she met through a friend. He was gentle and sweet, but difficult to live with because of his overwhelming trauma from Vietnam. After a few years, he gave her a baby, and soon after they parted. He continued to be Benjamin's dad.*

I was also remembering Jim, whom I loved, and who betrayed me, in service to his dream of living a lifetime in France. A friend had told me Jim had died of a heart attack a few years after I left Paris. I was feeling sad for him, sad for me, sad for Amy and Nick. When I finished the dishes I cleaned up the counter and saw in the corner a small strange object. I picked it up and examined it. Slowly, in amazement, I recognized it as a tiny pearl-and-diamond pendant that once hung from Jim's mother's necklace. He had given it to Amy years ago, while we still lived together in Paris.

When Amy came out of the bedroom, I showed it to her and asked, "Did you put this on the kitchen counter?"

She looked at it, surprised, and said, "No, I haven't seen that in years."

"Where did you keep it?" I asked.

"I don't even remember," she told me.

I looked at it in my hand and felt Jim's presence, caught up in the double emotions of realizing that this was a manifestation, a message, and of understanding that it meant that Jim was telling me that he cared. I couldn't find any other way to relate to that occurrence but to see it as a message from beyond the grave.

 CR

I was alone in my house in Mountaindale, in the Catskills. I heard a rustling sound in the cast-iron woodstove and knew that a bird had once again flown down the chimney. (There was one summer when several bluebirds a week would fly down the stovepipe and have to be rescued, eventually convincing me that the bluebird of happiness was, indeed, in my own backyard.) I had never rescued a bird from the stove by myself before, and I was frantically trying to figure out how to do it while the bird was frantically trying to get out of there.

Finally, I decided I would tape a garbage bag to the stove, open the door, and the bird would fly cooperatively into it and allow me to rescue it. With some effort I got a plastic bag taped around the double doors of the stove, and then confidently opened it. The bird flew out the open doors and right out of the bag, pulling the tape away with ease. (If I'd been more of an engineer I could have anticipated that.) It was a big bird, and it flew around the house, not a lot happier to be in its larger prison than it had been in the stove. I chased after it hopelessly, well aware that I was not equipped to catch a bird.

Finally, with a burst of good luck, I managed to herd the bird into the laundry room and shut the door. Then I called a friend at the ashram and begged him to come over and help me. In fifteen minutes he was there. We opened the door to the laundry room cautiously, expecting the bird to come zooming out. Nothing happened. We went in, shut the door behind us, and turned on the light. The laundry room had no windows. It had three walls of shelves, and a washer and dryer. In the back wall was a small exhaust fan with a grill over it and fan blades inside. We looked around, but no bird. We looked behind the boxes and large objects on the shelves, but no bird.

We examined the exhaust fan, but the grill in front of it would not allow passage of anything larger than a hummingbird. We looked again under and behind everything, and after half an hour we gave up. My friend left apologetically, hoping I wouldn't end up with a smelly corpse in a few days. I hoped so too. I looked repeatedly in the laundry room for several days after that, but the bird never reappeared. Unlike the bluebirds, I don't know what the message was, other than Strange Things Happen.

∞

I had just arrived back in Mountaindale for a few days' visit. I unpacked my bag and looked around, happy to be there again. I thought, "Oh, I hope I see a hummingbird. I haven't seen one in so long." Within fifteen minutes, I heard a tapping on the glass wall of the solarium. I went out to look, and there was a hummingbird, making his way along the glass front of the house, tapping on the windows as he went. I was ecstatic at having received a response so quickly. Then the same thing happened later—I was wishing I would see the blue heron that lived at our pond, and within a short while he appeared, flying from right to left in front of the house, his neck curved in its peculiar bend, looking like an Egyptian frieze. I was utterly content, knowing I was back in my magical domain.

∞

We were convinced that Harmonic Convergence, which occurred in August of 1987, would be a significant event, and we invited our old friends from the ashram to come and spend the time with us. Most of them ended up going to places like Mount Shasta or Haleakala, but two of our dear friends, Dougie and Luc, came to be with Amy and me. We decided we'd wake up early and watch the sun rise. We got up and went out to the front lawn where we had a good view of the eastern sky. As the sun touched the horizon we heard a rushing noise. A flock of geese flew in a straight line toward us, honking as they came. They were dots in the distance, getting bigger and bigger until at last they passed directly over our heads, honking and calling, and so low we could hear the rush of their wings. They were in a sinuous V, and I said, "It's the Feathered Serpent!"—the symbol of the Harmonic Convergence.

We spent the day chanting, meditating, and playing together, and toward evening the other three decided to go out to dinner. I didn't want to, and went outside to lie in the hammock while they got dressed. I was lying there reading when I felt something bump lightly but firmly against me under the hammock. I leaned over to try to see it, and it bumped again. It kept bumping and bumping me, gentle little nudges, as though to get my attention. Then a monarch butterfly appeared and flew around me, making a circle around the hammock, and bumping me from beneath every time it went under me. It did this for a while, and finally the others came out. I showed them the butterfly, and we all stood looking at it. It flew to Dougie and landed on his finger. It sat there a long while, and then flew to Luc. After a while it flew back to Dougie and landed on his third eye. Luc ran to get the video camera, and we taped the butterfly landing on each of us in turn for more than two hours. Finally, the other three got too hungry and decided to leave. I went back to the hammock, and they got in the car and left. The butterfly flew after them all the way down the drive. I thought it was gone, but when they turned onto the road it flew back to me, made a few more circles around the hammock and me, again bumping into me as it went underneath. Finally, it flew away, leaving me with no way to explain its visit, but overjoyed by the gift.

CR

I had been reading The Clan of the Cave Bear. In it, the main character, Ayla, is given a token by her totem animal. It seemed so wondrous to me—so satisfyingly material. I developed an intense *desire for a token from my totem. I went around thinking, "I want a token from my totem." At this same time I was trying to discover my relationship with Nityananda, Baba's successor guru, to whom Baba had given the name of his own guru. Was he my guru? Did he even know who I was? (Not that that matters—many people have received great blessings from Muktananda and other gurus without their knowing who those people were.) I was still wrapped up in the personal relationship I'd been fortunate enough to have with Baba, and I wanted it again. So my second mantra became, "Does he love me?"*

Those two thoughts were in my head for a few weeks. One day a friend came to visit from the ashram. We took a walk together down the hill in front of the house, and at the end of the grassy area, near the road, she stopped and said, "What's that?" I looked where she was pointing and saw a heart made of dirt. It was perfectly smooth, and was sitting up on the dirt around it, like an embossing. The heart was perfect. It was simply impossible for it to exist. I leaned over to see it better and discovered an iron heart in the dirt. The recent rain had washed the dirt into the heart and piled it up, like a cake in a cake form. I picked up the iron heart. It was rusty and flaking but intact. It had a perfect heart shape, except that it was open at the bottom, as though something else was supposed to get in or get out the tiny gap. We stared at it, unbelieving. It was clearly an intentional object, shaped for some use, but what? And how had it gotten there? I was blown away. I put it on my altar, where it remains.

ॐ

I was in New York City, where I'd gone to accompany Robert on a business trip. While he played the important lawyer with his clients, I was free to wander around the city. As I was getting dressed in our hotel room, I decided that I would test my new interest in the world beyond the one that is available to the senses. I said to myself, "Today I will see a paper hat." I walked out to wander around the city, something I've always loved doing in Paris and New York. Every time I turned a corner, I expected to see a paper hat. The one I had in mind was the sailor hat my uncle used to make for me by folding a sheet of newspaper into a shape that could be seen either as a hat or a sailboat.

I wandered all day but didn't see my hat. On the corner of Sixth Avenue, in the fifties, however, I saw a Viking. He was dressed in full Viking regalia, with a fur skin thrown over his shoulder, a domed helmet with horns sticking out the sides, a short skirt, and leather sandals wrapped around his bare legs. He was standing quietly, leaning on his spear. I stopped in my tracks at the strangeness of it. What was he doing there? He wasn't advertising anything. The thing that shook me up the most about this scene was that crowds of people were walking by him without so much as a glance. He paid no attention to them; they paid no attention to him. I finally concluded that he must appear on that corner a lot, and people were simply used to him. This was New York, after all.

So I went home disappointed, glad to have seen a Viking, but discouraged that I couldn't manifest my thoughts in the material world—not even enough to produce a paper hat. I had one of my frequent temporary lapses of faith.

A few weeks passed, and I went to visit my daughter at college. On this occasion, Amy and I were talking about some feelings that she had carried over from childhood. As we sat there, I heard a sharp, not loud but distinct, clicking sound. It registered in my awareness as something significant, and I turned to see what it was. Next to me on the floor was a little square of masking tape. It was about a half-inch-square, and had one torn edge, as though it had been torn off a roll. The edge had been pushed up from the corner so that it was folded diagonally, in a one-stroke fold, giving it the shape of a paper hat. It was an utterly simple, utterly complete paper hat. I held it in the palm of my hand and stared. I had never been so in awe of an object in my life. This was my manifestation, not just lucking into someone's coincidental paper hat on the street, but a paper hat that had been created for me, somewhere else, in some other world, in answer to my wish and to send me a message I would never forget. The simplicity of the form was beyond genius. It was divine. It is my greatest treasure.

Many years after these incidents, I heard on public radio that the musician Moondog had died. They were doing a retrospective of his music, which was fascinating, original, liberated, and lighthearted. I was enjoying listening, when they began to talk about his life. The commentator said that Moondog used to dress up as a Viking and hang around on street corners in New York. Thanks, Moondog.

CR

After my second bout with breast cancer, in 1984, I went to Hawaii for two months to be healed and re-energized by the spirit of the place. Friends, fellow-ashramites, lived on the slopes of Haleakala, and they helped me to find a place to stay on Maui and were open and generous in their hospitality. I had dinner with them frequently, and spent time with their family. It was a magical time, and maybe it did heal me, because despite many recurrences of cancer, I'm still here.

We were together one day, and I had smoked marijuana, which I did daily while I was there—who wouldn't? I have always appreciated marijuana's ability to give me profound insights into my life. I treated it as a sacred substance. I never abused it by using it casually or for partying. In return, it gave me a depth of understanding about myself and the world that I had no other way of accessing. My friend teased me regularly because I would only smoke once a day. He was a very far-out guy, a real saddhu (holy man). His wife was lovely and warm, and on this day she was cooking rice for our dinner while I sat on the couch. She uttered a cry of dismay, and I asked her what was wrong.

"I burned the rice," she said.

In my dreamy state I tried to comfort her. "It doesn't matter," I said. *"I like burned rice."*

She was comforted, and I sat in an inward state, trance-like. Gradually I noticed that I was rubbing the thumb and forefinger of my right hand together, over and over. There was something between my fingers. I looked at it. In my hand was a grain of burned rice.

Hawaii was magical for me in many ways. On my birthday I walked the few blocks from my rented house to the beach. It was evening and the beach was deserted. I walked down to the water and spotted something on the sand. When I got close, I bent to pick it up. It was a lei of champa flowers. For my birthday. I looked up and out at the water, and at that moment a whale leapt out of the water to the end of his flukes, and dove back in. The sun set in front of me and the moon rose behind me, and I was caught in a web of earth magic. For my birthday.

I loved walking on the beach on Maui. My house was close to a long strand of sand, and I walked there often. It was never crowded, but often I chose to go at times when it was empty. On the day I'm remembering, I was walking along the beach as waves lapped gently near my feet. I came across a praying mantis struggling to stand on its feet in the sand. Every time it got a foothold, a wavelet would wash up and catch it, knocking it over. I watched it for a minute and then walked on. I got a few steps away when something grabbed me, as insistent as a hand. I suddenly knew I had to go back. I turned and went back to the mantis.

As I stood there looking down at it, its eyes swiveled up and looked at me. In my mind I heard it say, "Are you going to leave me here?" I knew that I couldn't, but at the same time I was totally freaked out by the idea of picking it up. I had a life-long revulsion toward bugs, and I couldn't bring myself to touch it. So I went in search of something to pick it up with—preferably a long stick. All I could find was a smooth, round black rock a little bigger than a golf ball—one of those volcanic rocks that you find in Hawaii, the jewels of the goddess Pele. I took the rock back to the mantis and, bending over, I held it out. Without hesitation, the mantis climbed onto the rock, one leg at a time, like someone getting into a lifeboat. I could feel the sharp points of its tiny claws on my fingers. I shuddered, but I held on.

Once the mantis was on board, I carried it gingerly over to a fringe of bushes at the back of the beach, and found a leaf to put it on. I held the rock next to the leaf, and the mantis climbed off. I dropped the rock and went off on my walk, but later I thought, what was I thinking? I should have tried to communicate with it. I went back to try to find it, but it was gone. It changed me, though. I vowed to see insects as creatures, conscious like all the others. I'm not very good at that, but I make an effort. Maybe this experience in Hawaii prepared the way for the visit of the monarch butterfly some years later.

☙

Periodically in India, often to commemorate a holiday devoted to one of the gods, but sometimes for an event such as the guru's birthday, a yagna (ceremonial fire) was held. Amy and I were there on the occasion of a yagna dedicated to the god Vishnu, of whom Krishna is a form. The preparations for a yagna are elaborate and impressive, and I felt privileged to be able to witness the procedure. The mandap, a permanent open-air, tent-like structure on the grounds of the ashram, had at its center a large fire pit. Around it were floor areas that could accommodate many hundreds of people sitting cross-legged on the ground.

The event started one morning with a group of Indian women in saris on their knees, rubbing the entire floor of the mandap with dried cow dung, a ritual that consecrates the space. There is nothing disgusting about this—the dung is dry and fragrant and completely unobjectionable, even to my fastidious Western point of view. Around that time, we would begin to see the Brahmin priests walking around the grounds of the ashram, busy with tasks. They were sent for from other parts of India for the occasion. One of the tasks, which I was fortunate to participate in, was the cleaning of the wooden spoons that were used to pour ghee on the fire. The spoons were pulled out of storage—a set of about seven long-handled spoons, hand-carved, and each one a different shape. Some were shaped like stirring spoons, one was like a little ladle, some had trenches carved into them to allow the liquid ghee to pour out into the fire. The spoons were caked with ghee when I got them, and it was my job to restore them to cleanliness. I rubbed and rubbed, as energetically as I would have rubbed Aladdin's lamp, and feeling just as lucky. The spoons glowed with the patina of the ghee.

Other ashramites were piling up wood near the edge of the mandap, to burn in the fire. The Brahmin priests were gathering and preparing the offerings that would be made to the fire: ghee, incense, sandalwood paste, and ground-up gold and jewels. The day of the yagna people were out early in the morning, decorating the mandap with strands of flowers—red, white, and pink carnations; marigolds; and champa—strung in garlands and hung thickly behind Baba's chair. The women at the ashram dressed themselves in saris—something I learned to do for myself but never enjoyed. The saris were gorgeous, though—heavy silks bordered with designs in gold, and each one different. The sight of all of us dressed like Indian princesses added festivity and importance to the occasion.

Amy and I arrived together and were given seats in a front row, an honor that Baba almost always bestowed on me, for no reason that I could understand. We put down our meditation mats and pillows and sat cross-legged on the floor to wait. When most of us were seated, there was the usual stir that preceded the arrival of the Guru—something like the cool wind that stirs up when a storm is coming. Baba arrived in full regalia—orange silk robes and an orange silk shawl thrown over his shoulder. He sat on his orange silk chair in front of the curtain of flowers, and we began to chant. When our chant stopped the Brahmin priests took over. One of them picked up his fire-making tools and went to the center of the mandap. He had a flat-topped wooden stick with a bowl carved out of the center, a pointed round stick with grooves cut in the sides, and *a length of rope. In the depression in the flat stick were some wisps of straw. Accompanied by the deep-throated, hypnotic chanting of the Brahmin priests, he squatted in front of his tools and stuck the pointed stick in the hole. While another priest held the stick in place, he wrapped the rope around it, and turned the stick back and forth as fast as he could by pulling first one end and then the other of the rope. The stick twirled and we held our breath. I have seen that procedure performed many times, and it never fails to produce a high measure of suspense as we wait long minutes for the first wisp of smoke to rise. When it does, the priest blows on the straw until the fire glows, and then he holds up the stick containing the fire, and the crowd goes wild.*

When the priest has fanned the glowing spark to a flame he pours the fire into the fire pit and adds fuel. The fire pit is about four feet deep and four feet on a side, and it will eventually be filled with logs, as the flames are fed. As he prepares the fire, the other priests, four or five of them, dressed in orange lunghis *and bare-chested, continue to chant. I learned that they start by chanting the name of the place, the date, the name of the sponsor of the* yagna *and the name of the god to whom it is dedicated. Then they chant scripture. There is a long chant associated with* yagnas, *and they chant it and chant it until the end of the* yagna, *sometimes three or four days later. As they chant they hold the wooden spoons and ladle ghee onto the fire. When the ghee hits the fire, it flares up out of the pit and shoots sparks up toward the ceiling. They also throw in logs, and handfuls of black material from what looks like a pile of coarsely ground dark chocolate, only oilier. This is the mixture of precious substances that are offered to the flames. Each time they add something to the fire, they chant in unison,* "Swaha!" *("I offer it!"). Soon the atmosphere is thick with smoke, the smells of burning ghee and sandalwood, the deep-voiced sounds of the chant, and a sacred vibration you could cut with a knife. Given some free time, I would rather be there than almost any other place on earth.*

Amy and I sat there drinking it in. At one point I turned to her and said, "Do you hear the flute?" She nodded yes. There was a beautiful flute accompaniment to the chant, which was a very unusual thing. I looked around for the flute player and couldn't see one. I whispered to Amy, "Who's playing the flute?" She looked around and couldn't find anyone either. I whispered to my neighbor on the other side, "Who's playing the flute?"

She whispered back, "What flute?

"You don't hear a flute?"

"No."

"Now—do you hear that?"

"No."

I turned back to Amy and told her. She asked her neighbor, who also didn't hear it. We decided to signal each other when we heard it, raising our fingers together each time the flute played. There was no doubt that we were both hearing the same thing, and that the others around us were not hearing it. It was an unusually beautiful sound, and it went on all day for us, until the closing mantras. *The amazing thing is that the* yagna *was dedicated to Krishna, the flute player. What we were hearing has a name in Sanskrit. It's called* nada—*sound that is not made by physical means.*

I had experienced nada *once before. My first year at the ashram I was living in my new house and therefore didn't follow Baba to a warmer place for the winter, as most of the ashramites did. A skeleton crew stayed behind to keep the ashram going. Most of the building was shut down, since there was only a handful of people—maybe ten or twelve. We had programs, though, where we got together in the evening and chanted and meditated together. The large meditation hall was shut down, so a portion of the ashram restaurant had been blocked off and rugs put on the floor to make a cozy little chanting space. I would drive to the ashram for the program and join the chant. One evening, we were chanting one of the beautiful chants we did regularly, when I started hearing a wonderfully complex drumbeat. I always chanted with my eyes closed, but I wanted to know who the exceptionally gifted drummer was. I opened my eyes* and looked around at the small assembly of chanters, but I didn't see a drummer. I closed my eyes and heard the drumming again. I opened my eyes—still no drummer that I could see.

At the end of the program I went up to the manager of the ashram and asked, "Was there a drummer?"

He said, "No, did you hear one?"

I said I had.

He smiled. "Hearing some nada, huh?"

There is something I have noticed every time I came in contact with these otherworldly phenomena. The drumming was remarkably complex and noticeably attractive. The flute playing was unusually beautiful. My best description would be that they were like heavenly music. They drew my attention because of their quality, not just because I didn't expect them to be there. The appearance of the paper hat had something of that same quality—I heard a tiny sound and I knew without any doubt that it had significance, that I needed to pay attention to it, as though it were accompanied by a sacred vibration that gets your attention in some way you can't explain.

At the end of the Vishnu yagna I was given another gift, somewhat less dramatic, but still precious to me. Whenever there was a pause in the ceremony—in the evening, for example, or at mealtimes—it was the custom to walk around the fire pit in a clockwise direction, eventually adding up to 108 times. I loved doing that, and I did it every chance I could get. At the end of the yagna I spent a while walking around the fire pit, enjoying the sacred atmosphere in the mandap and feeling blissful. At one point I was three-quarters of the way around when I saw a plume of white smoke arise from the pit. It rose straight up, and then curved and came toward me. When it was over my head, it curved downward and surrounded me in a pillar of smoke. I stood still, in awe and gratitude. It doesn't sound like much, but it was.

CR

This story is the worst (because it demonstrated my frustration, and my boldness in demanding something from the Guru), and also the best. I was in India, hanging out with my friend Luc. Both of us had made dutiful efforts to meditate regularly in the meditation cave, and we were both complaining at our lack of success. It was common around the ashram to hear stories of profound meditation experiences, of visions of gods or cosmic expansion of consciousness— all kinds of magical experiences that I envied energetically. It was also a practice at the evening programs at the ashram in New York to have a talk given by an ashramite. These talks were full of "experiences" and aroused my jealousy and my dissatisfaction with the progress of my spiritual journey. I told Luc I was disgusted—I couldn't meditate, and I never had any visions. He sympathized. I told him I was going to go into the little town a mile away and visit the temple dedicated to Baba's guru, Bhagawan Nityananda. There I would DEMAND an experience. Luc said he would go with me, and ask for one too. I decided to put a deadline on my demand—ten days away, New Year's Eve.

We walked the mile to town in the morning heat. The town was one block long, and was lined with commerce—open-fronted sheds that housed the tailor, the clothing shop, the tiny general store, and the restaurant where it was common to see a Brahman bull ambling through the narrow aisle and examining the contents of the six or so tables. At the end of the street was the Nityananda temple, and that's where we went. In front were broad marble steps leading up to the door. The steps were strewn with shoes left by people who had gone inside. (I never heard of anyone's shoes being stolen from a temple in India.) We left our shoes and went in.

The temple is made of marble, and is cool, high-ceilinged, and decorated with garlands. In front is a white marble railing, and behind it, on a pedestal, sits a statue of Nityananda, cross-legged and hung with garlands. Every evening the priests of the temple performed arati, *the evening prayer, waving a lit oil lamp in front of the statue and chanting. At the hour when we were there, the temple was quiet and almost empty. A few people sat in meditation on the marble floor. Luc and I separated, since women sit on one side and men on the other. We sat there for a while, and I made my petition to my Guru's guru, specifying my deadline. Then we walked home.*

We checked in with each other daily, but had nothing to report. Then, the day before my deadline, I was lying on my bed taking a nap. I half-woke from my nap, in a state of such ecstatic bliss that it woke me up. I was awake, but definitely not in normal waking consciousness. I couldn't think or talk or move—all I could do was utter profound sighs of ecstasy. There was no content to the ecstatic bliss—it was cosmic. But down at my feet I could see my life proceeding from left to right, like a tiny caravan. It moved slowly from one side to the other, an endless stream of the events of my life, unrolling at my feet. I knew in those moments that it was totally irrelevant. It was happening, but it had no importance. I reported my experience to Luc. I considered it a spectacular success. He was happy for me, but a little put out.

BEADED BAGS

My children have children now. *I tell people that having grandchildren is the reward you get for having children. I waited many years for grandchildren. Having had my own kids young, I expected to be a young grandmother, but that's not how it happened. Both my children had their children late. For a long time there were none, and then suddenly my daughter-in-law, Lauren, was pregnant and three months later, Amy. Babies rained from the skies. Nikola was the first, then Benjamin. I always felt that Benjamin didn't want to be born until he was sure that Nikola would be there. After a year, Madison came—my first granddaughter, probably my only granddaughter. The three of them love each other fervently, and wait impatiently for the times when we are all together. One of my favorite sights is watching them run to hug each other when they first get together. I always jump out of the car and run to be there so I won't miss it. Now there is a new baby, Julian. He is exactly like Jonathan at his age—sunny and smiling. I count myself fortunate to have this golden crop of children.*

When my mother died her beaded bags came to me. They are exquisite—covered with tiny beads in twining floral patterns, lined in creamy satin, with jeweled clasps and gold-chain or beaded shoulder straps. She must have bought them in Paris soon after the end of the war. I kept one and gave one to my daughter, along with my mother's almost-up-to-the-shoulder white satin gloves, still in their silky cellophane bag. My daughter was electrified, and seized them. When next I visited, she had made a shrine to my mother on a vertical wooden beam in her Vermont kitchen, the bag hung on a hook with the gloves hanging full length beneath it, and over all a picture of my mother in a white dress, smiling in her 1950s harlequin glasses and blond-dyed hair.

I marveled again at how this woman who was so unable to give me, her first-born, only daughter, her love had been so lavish with it to my children. She adored them, her only grandchildren, and held nothing back. Their tender relationship made me doubt at times my own truth—was this the woman who had not a single soft touch, tender word, loving kiss for me?

I am third in a line of three grandmothers, beginning with my mother's mother, who spoke only Yiddish and who therefore never spoke to me. My mother told me many times that her mother was an angel, but I never understood what she meant. Now I reflect that after seven children and the nine grandchildren who came before me, she had probably run out of the energy it would have taken for her love to jump the barrier and reach over to touch me.

The second grandmother is my mother, who was a different woman for my children than she was for me, and I applaud the good fortune that let her open and experience the love they had for each other.

The third grandmother is me, and not having experienced any role model, I have had to create my own image of who a grandmother is. The loving part is easy—each child comes with his or her own fund of love, and we share that abundance together. The learning part is: What do I mean to them? What does it mean to a child to have an adoring grandmother? I take my cues from the shrine in my daughter's kitchen.

ૐ TWENTY
Leaving

THOUGH I NO LONGER WENT to the ashram, I did not think of leaving the house that Baba had twice blessed for me. It had become my own personal ashram, and I now planned to continue my spiritual path with only Baba as my guide. This decision ended up having a profound and unanticipated effect on me. Whereas before I had looked to Baba for guidance and was dependent on him for my spiritual understanding, I now opened myself to messages from any part of my life. In other words, the whole world had become the guru, and I became open to the guidance that came in the form of the events of my life, or the people who came into it—without requiring them to be spiritually advanced teachers. Dreams were a big part of the spiritual teachings I acknowledged, as was my own inner voice, which sometimes told me things I didn't know I'd been thinking about.

I continued to stay in my beloved house, where memories of Baba, and even Baba's *shakti*, surrounded me. The few friends I had left at the ashram were often afraid to come and see me. My closest friends, who were not followers of Chidvilasananda, moved away to Texas, Canada, California, and other far-away places. I missed the ashram life, but I considered that it was over, and the physical presence of the ashram ten minutes from my house did nothing to revive it.

I enjoyed the solitude and spaciousness of country living, and the connection with nature that it provided. The surrounding area had nothing much to offer, though. Baba often chose run-down areas in which to establish his ashrams, and this one was no exception. It was a physically beautiful spot, but the beauty was disguised and hidden by the relics of a former resort colony that had gone to ruin when the trains stopped running from New York City, and cheap flights to Europe lured the vacation trade away from the Catskill Mountains. The surrounding towns were derelict and lackluster affairs, offering almost no cultural or even commercial amenities. Occasional trips to New York City provided our only distraction. I loved the absence of temptation that was a benefit of this way of life, but eventually I realized that I had become accustomed to living in a wide and rich community of seekers, and I felt a lack.

Living in that place had been a spiritual journey for me. It was my cave in the Himalayas, a retreat from worldly life, a place where I could be in silence for days at a time and go for a few weeks without seeing anyone. Gradually, it had become a place of peace, and others who came there noticed. For me it deepened my relationship with the earth, with the animal and plant kingdoms, and with the guru who gave me the gift of the vibration that made that place what it was. I thought I would never leave there, but Baba died and everything changed.

I decided to leave, without knowing where to go.

I knew I was going toward community, though. It was my reason for leaving. It was around 1988 or '89, and I spoke to my friends in California, saying that it would be wonderful if we could all live together again, in an intentional community.

I saw a program on the evening news that described a new type of community called cohousing, and I thought, "That's exactly what I've been dreaming up." It described communities that had been started in Denmark, where people owned their own houses, which were clustered together in a village-like setting. They had a Common House for shared activities and meals together several times a week, cooked by a rotating team of community members. I wanted to live that way.

My friends in California said, "Yes, great." I knew they weren't coming back to the Catskills, because I'd been unsuccessful in my efforts to persuade them not to leave. So Amy and I went to California. We rented a large motor home and five of us, representing the rest, set out to ride up the coast from San Francisco to Portland, looking for a place where we could agree to settle and create our own community. The trip was a blast—we went wherever one of us thought there might be a place worth looking at. We stopped every couple of hours for snacks ("Time for a snack, isn't it?") and parked at night wherever we could find a space big enough for our huge rambling home on wheels. We went to Grass Valley and Santa Rosa and Mount Shasta and Ashland and Eugene, Oregon. From there we drove up the coast to Portland. All along the way my friends kept saying, "This is great. Someday we're surely going to live together." By the end of the trip I understood that they were not ready to commit themselves yet. I went home knowing that I didn't want to live in community "someday." I wanted it now. I just didn't know where or how.

Summer at my home in the Catskills was an ecstatic time, partly because of the beauty of the place, and the wild animals that came out of hiding, but mostly because of the wild blueberry bushes. There were literally thousands of them. They were everywhere, covering many parts of the land. They were old and venerable grandfathers of bushes, some as tall as eight to ten feet, and they bore blueberries in abundance. The berries on each bush had a distinct flavor, some sweet, some tart, some mild, and some intense. The berry sizes ranged from tiny to prize-winning, and there was a range of colors, including striped. It was my great pleasure to go out early in the morning and pick blueberries for breakfast. I would tie a container around my neck so I could pick with both hands, and gather blueberries to eat and some to freeze. It pleased me that there were so many berries I didn't have to worry about the birds eating them. I once saw a fox nibbling off the lowest branches of a bush. He was welcome to his harvest. Even the Japanese beetles, which flock to blueberries, couldn't make a dent in the abundance.

The summer after our West Coast trip, I found myself picking blueberries and singing the same song, over and over. I had recently seen the movie *Bagdad Cafe*, a wonderful and haunting film. I was singing the theme song that plays through many scenes of the movie. It was "I-I-I am calling you." I sang it and sang it. I knew what I was calling for. I was calling for community. I didn't know where to look for it, so I sent my call out into the ether on the wings of song.

On August 9, I had a dream. I dreamed that I entered a room that was full of people. As I went in I realized that a group was being called together.

As it happened, a group was being called together. The day after my dream, an ad went into the local paper serving Northampton and Amherst, Massachusetts. The ad asked for people who were interested in starting a community together. My call had been answered, but I had no way of knowing it yet.

I spent a lot of time thinking about where to go. At some point I remembered my experience on the West Coast. What I remembered was that every time we came to a quaint little town that resembled the New England towns I was familiar with, I would say, "This looks nice. I could live here." It occurred to me that maybe I wanted to live in New England. By now, Jonathan was married and living in Connecticut. His interests in music and electronics had meshed, and he ended up with a recording studio in a little town near Hartford. I asked Jonathan what, in his opinion, were the nicest towns in New England. Brattleboro and Northampton, he told me.

I had been to Brattleboro, Vermont, once. Amy and Jonathan were familiar with it because their father, Dan, had a vacation house nearby, and they had spent summers with him there in the years after our divorce. I knew nothing about Northampton except that I had visited it once, as a teenager, after being accepted to Smith College. I hadn't thought much of it then.

I now felt I had a plan. That fall Amy and I made a trip to have a look at Northampton and Brattleboro. Driving into Northampton I was captivated by its newfound charm. The town had changed a lot since I last saw it and had become a cosmopolitan little backwater with first-rate crafts stores, an art supply store, restaurants and cafés, two art movie houses, and a lively Main Street. (We went to a movie at one of the theaters, an old opera house that had been converted to a movie theater, and were amazed and enchanted to see that the candies they offered were bars of Lindt chocolate, and the popcorn was made with real butter.) We stayed for a day and then went on to Brattleboro. Amy felt at home there. The trip propelled us into our own decisions. Amy moved to Brattleboro that fall, and in December I moved to Northampton.

In January of 1990, when I had been living in Northampton for a month, Amy called me in some excitement. She told me she had been to a party the day before, and she'd overheard someone talking about a cohousing group that was just forming. She gave me his phone number and told me to call him. I did call him, and he told me about two groups in the Northampton area that were starting up. I called them both, and one called me back. It was my group.

I went to their next meeting and every meeting after that. When I showed up there were seven people, in various stages of commitment, who had been meeting for several months. Their membership had been stuck at seven for a while, and they were delighted to add me to their number. I pitched headlong into the formation stage of a cohousing community based in Amherst, Massachusetts, twenty minutes drive from Northampton, an activity that was to occupy me for the next five years, as the group grew and solidified and eventually manifested its vision.

WHO ARE WE?
(Our Cohousing Community)

WE LIVE TOGETHER AND KEEP *our common home going.*

We each have our own house, but we share a common house, a garden, a studio and workshop, and all our land.

We eat together twice a week.

We celebrate the big events together—weddings, leavings, arrivals, births—no deaths yet.

We meet together monthly. Some of us habitually attend our meetings. Some habitually do not.

Some do a huge amount of the common work. Some do not. For the most part, we allow that. I find that admirable, because it suggests that we know that people contribute in different ways. (For example, although we don't honor our critics, they do an important service. And it's a hard job, very unappreciated.)

Some of us want closeness. Some do not. Some want emotional openness. Some do not. This is a big, hot, unresolved issue: WHAT IS COMMUNITY (to me)? I am just discovering the answer for myself. Community is what we have here. It's about as disappointing as my family was. And it's as good as life. The disappointments, I think, are just concepts of the way I expected it to be. It's not the little things that make community. It's the overall feeling.

It occurs to me we may all end up friends here, or at least with many friends, closer to some than to others, but with relationships with everyone. Sort of like those movies you see of small towns where everyone knows everyone else and feels something for them, and you think, "Oh, that's the way it should be," or "I'd like to live there." Somewhere along the way we lost that feeling of connectedness and now have to try to recreate it. Cohousing is like a town intentionally building itself all at once, instead of happening gradually. In those towns and villages everyone stayed put—the relationships were lifelong. Cohousing is an attempt to create that. In the old villages it was harder to leave. We choose to stay, even though we don't have to.

We look around at each other and it's like an arranged marriage. Who is this person? Who are these people? Why am I going to spend the rest of my life with him/her/them? Is that who I would have chosen? If you don't surrender the choosing you start to think you could have chosen better. But villages don't grow that way. The miracle is that a number of people who were randomly selected and don't start out with a lot in common grow to love each other—in fact, to love each other unconditionally for who we are, in spite of quarrels and issues and hurts and disappointments. Like a good marriage.

‏ TWENTY-ONE

The Last Dance

BERNIE SIEGEL GAVE UP HIS cancer practice in favor of spreading his wisdom more widely, so I found a holistic doctor and saw him for checkups. I had a mammogram, and the doctor wrote me and told me it looked fine, but the radiologist wanted to see my previous one. The previous one was at a hospital in New Haven, so I called them or wrote (I don't remember which) asking to have it sent. Then I forgot about it. It looked okay anyway, I thought, so they just wanted to check it. Six months went by and the doctor wrote to me reminding me to have my mammogram sent. I called New Haven again and this time they sent it. To my astonishment, the radiologist told me it looked like I had a recurrence. In my meeting with him, he told me the mammogram had looked suspicious to him, and that's why he wanted to check the previous one. I was floored. It looked to me like there was a lot of serious miscommunication going on.

It *was* a recurrence. Against my new surgeon's advice, I chose to have another lumpectomy. It had to be done twice, because the first didn't have clean margins. At this point I knew the dance was getting too fast for me. I needed some help. It was then that a friend gave me information about a doctor in New York who offered the Kelley Program to his cancer patients. This time I decided to try it.

The Kelley Program is a demanding, even grueling, metabolic program designed to kill the cancer cells in your body. It involves an unbelievable numbers of capsules—about one hundred and fifty—taken throughout the day at meals, between meals, and in the middle of the night. I thought the macrobiotic program was difficult, but this one was breaking new ground. I lived on a schedule dictated by the Program, and there were only a few hours of the day when I wasn't doing one or another of the things I was required to do. I told friends it was like having a baby, and the baby was me.

Without knowing why, I believed in what I was doing. A large part of my belief I credit to Dr. Gonzalez, who oversaw the program. On my initial visit he met with Amy and me for several hours on two consecutive days and explained the whole thing. He radiated confidence in what he was asking me to do. It impressed me greatly that he was following the Program himself, not because he had cancer but because he believes it keeps you healthy. I was pretty sure there weren't any doctors who choose to do chemotherapy because they think it's good for you.

I stuck to the Program for six years, during which time I had no further recurrences. I finally had to stop taking the supplements because I developed a swallowing problem so intense that I experienced it as worse than cancer. It eventually made it impossible for me to keep taking the supplements. It's now nineteen years since my last cancer operation and thirty-three years since the first.

I don't know how the Kelley Program works. It worked for me, and I know others it has worked for. I also know one it didn't work for. I know people who think Dr. Gonzalez is unscrupulous or a quack. For me, he is a hero—a doctor brave enough to offer an alternative, despite the opposition of the medical community, and to offer his patients hope and support. I don't know if it's the placebo effect that's at work. If it is, that's fine with me. A knowledgeable friend told me the placebo effect has about the same rate of success in cancer as chemotherapy. But I don't think that's all there is to it. I know there are other clinics that offer hope but not a lot of success. I suspect the Kelley Program really does kill cancer cells, and that many people have their lives extended by it. But I can't prove it. It's just my belief.

Cancer has been a great teacher for me. If for nothing else, the need to look death in the face leads to changes that can't be attained in other ways. I've heard many cancer patients say that life became more precious for them after they knew they had cancer. I think life is always precious to us, but we become more aware of it when there's a distinct possibility that we are going to die.

I explored many different approaches to healing on my journey. I did drawings, visualizations, I learned trance induction, and studied shamanism. I changed my relationship to the people close to me—I paid more attention to my own needs and stopped trying so hard to make everyone else happy. I think all of these approaches had an effect, on the assumption that cancer is not simply the growth of cells that appears in people chosen at random to undergo the experience, but has a lot to do with the growth and development of the person whose body is manifesting the cancer. I hear people complain that they are being held responsible for their illness, and blamed. I think the emphasis is wrong in that view. A potentially fatal illness is an opportunity to look at life, to make a closer and more meaningful relationship to how you got to be you and where you might want to go from here. And I believe that making a relationship with death can be as rewarding as making one with life. We are none of us going to be survivors in the long run. I learned to include death in my life. I found myself walking two paths—one towards life and one towards death. Each path gives meaning and value to the other.

It's a great mystery who lives and who dies. You see people on television grappling with it all the time, after an accident or a hurricane or other disasters that take lives. People are shaken when they survive and someone else doesn't. Sometimes they feel guilty—survivor's guilt—and can't get over it. Soldiers feel it. People who give their lives for others are celebrated as heroes. To me that's a hint that the point is not whether you live or die, but to become conscious of your life and to choose how to live it. I think we know when we're doing something with our lives that means something to us. I think when we don't our bodies find ways to tell us—to wake us up.

I am immensely grateful to have survived my cancer. I've reached an age that people refer to as elderly, despite the cancer. What it did for me is start me on the journey of making friends with death. As I grow older I know more and more surely that death is an important part of life—not an ending, but another adventure. I know that it means letting go of this life and the identity that goes with it, but I've had some practice in doing that now, and it's not so scary any more. Though I'm not there yet, I suspect that when I am facing death head on, I will be comforted by having practiced beforehand.

Death sings its siren song to me
In the stillness of the afternoon I listen
Immobilized, not breathing, as one listens to the heart fluttering
*   within*
It sings its songs to me, strange twanging sounds

THE LAST DANCE

Like Indian music, dividing time into its infinite fractions
And distant, oh so distant,
But drawing nearer.

❧ TWENTY-TWO

Growing Old

Y ES, EVEN HERE, IN AMERICA, there are advantages to growing old. Not, as in some cultures, an increase in prestige and authority, nor the guarantee of being looked after when the need arises. The advantages I've discovered are internal, and nonetheless welcome for that. For one thing, now that I'm in my seventies, I've noticed an ever-increasing ability to look past myself to a bigger picture. Also, an increasing dispassion—my needs and desires have become smaller as the years flow by. Some have been fulfilled, some abandoned, some forgotten. I look back at them the way a boat looks back at its wake. The waves are smaller around and ahead of me. The body encounters new difficulties, but the mind and heart enter calmer waters. Since I believe that the body is just a vehicle for who we really are, that's OK with me. Aging cars need more fixing, but they can still run.

The people around me speak of memory loss as a decline they associate with aging. It's not like that for me, though I certainly remember less than I did when I was younger. I forget words I know, or it takes me ten minutes to remember Charlton Heston's name, and I not only forget the plot and details of almost every movie I've seen, I often can't remember whether I've seen it.

When I was in my thirties, I used to forget where I had put my keys. I have never had a good memory for the names of people I have just met, and I think that's common. (I attribute it to the stress of wondering, unconsciously, what kind of impression you are making as you encounter the stranger and are told his or her name.) I used to carry around in my conveniently located brain the telephone numbers of all my friends and acquaintances, as well as all the places I regularly did business with. Now I use a personal phone book for that storage. The numbers gradually faded from my brain.

I used to be famous in the tiny circle of my family for being able to quote, accurately and verbatim, conversations between me and others. It's a skill I no longer have, and I miss it; but on the other hand I used it almost always to prove to someone that I was right, and somehow, with age, that need has become less urgent.

The most striking things I forget now are old hurts. As I sit in the sting of the wounds of conflict, I can feel the memory of those moments slipping away from me, like a time-lapse photograph of a skin wound healing. The cut closes, the skin knits together and scabs over, and by the end of the day you can hardly see where the scar is. By the next day the memory has sunk deep into the cellar rooms of my brain, packed in a box and marked with a label in case I ever need to retrieve it. I have let go of a lot of emotional turmoil that way. I don't regret not being able (or not choosing) to remember today why I was mad at my daughter yesterday. The past is not always worth remembering, especially when you have reached an age where you are no longer putting yourself together by accretion. I pretty much know myself now, and I don't need to hold on to the events in my life and turn them over and over and figure out how they fit into who I think of as me. I'm as me as I'm ever going to be, and in fact I think I'm going in the other direction. At my age I want to be less me, to lighten up and become less solid, more fluid. I want to flow in and around and through events, and to let them flow through me, not hold on to them. Even the good ones, the praise or admiration I occasionally receive—I notice them receding almost as soon as they are received. I figure I am practicing my approach to the void.

The result of all this is that I am thoroughly enjoying my old age—to the extent that one can enjoy anything as challenging and complicated as life. I hear people speaking of the inevitable decline they are going to experience as they grow old, and I want to shake them up and ask them how they are going to make room for things to become better if they are expecting them to get worse. I find my present life more relaxing, more full of wisdom, more in tune with the wonder of the earth, less anxiety-ridden, and less disturbed by the bumps and intrusions engendered by encounters with other people.

When I was young I was full of anxiety, trying to discover who I was, trying to figure out what to do and whom to do it with, trying to be the best at something. I was buffeted by the needs of the body and the yearnings created by my ignorance of life. Now I know what it is I don't need to know, and the day-to-day events of life seem less compelling. They pass before me like scenes from a movie, and unless they ring a bell, they fade and recede and are soon forgotten. The songs of my heart are louder now.

The things that stay with me stay for a reason. I think this is how life plans it for us—we come into the world in a cloud of spirit, and need to be acclimatized to the physical world. We spend our childhood doing that, acquiring mastery and figuring out what we are going to be when we grow up. Then life whizzes by, and suddenly we are old and on our way back to where we came from. But at my age I have figured out that I can just let it happen, that I don't have to be in control, that there are bigger forces at work. I let go and enjoy the ride.

ক TWENTY-THREE
Final Thoughts

L IKE MANY PEOPLE, I SPENT the first many years of my life trying to find out who I was, or alternatively, trying to become
somebody, preferably me. In my early years I was indelibly
marked by the environment I lived in. My mother's corrosive,
non-stop dissatisfaction with me put a box around me and
choked off what might have been the expression of who I was
born to be. I was afraid to do or say anything, for fear of the
inevitable attack. I had a great love for reading, drawing, and
thinking. I drew on everything I could get my hands on, which
meant the pages of my books and the backs of envelopes. I remember my aunts asking me at the age of three what I wanted
to be. I always answered "an artist." I drew in the margins of
all my notebooks, right through college (and even now), and
was always criticized for it, until I became self-conscious about
it and tried to hide it. I saw that others saw it as messy, but I
couldn't stop. Under criticism I became less and less able to
draw and paint, until finally I stopped, and didn't begin again
until halfway through psychoanalysis, in my thirties.

When I sat down to read, my mother told me, always, that
I should be doing something else. Usually it was go outside,

but sometimes it was play with other kids. She said I read too much. She and I were so different. She was possessed of abundant energy, exacerbated by nervous energy that made her restless and needy, unable to sit still. I was, and still am, slow-moving and reflective, more focused on inner life and not in need of much outward activity. I suspect this came about partly in reaction to my mother, whose fast pace and frenzied activity level felt profoundly uncomfortable to me. When I sit down to read now I still bite my nails. Somewhere deep inside is the little girl expecting her mother to see her and attack.

My best defense was to be invisible, a trait I perfected and am still a champion at.

It took six years of psychoanalysis for me to truly discover myself, and to become quite simply who I felt myself to be. Until then I was ruled by a chaotic blend of emotions, rules, avoidance strategies, fears, and inertia. Every creative thought had to make its way through this obstacle course in order to manifest. Most of those impulses died in the labyrinth, unable to find their way out. My inner, creative, and joyous self was a prisoner in the labyrinth, in constant conflict between my emotions, my fears, my desires, and my need to be invisible. During analysis I lay on the couch, having complete responsibility for everything that took place there. Either I talked, or nothing happened. I lay stuck for long periods on end, facing the paradoxes of my inner being and despairing. I learned I had to have the courage and determination to speak anyway, and in doing that, I began to unravel the profound mystery of who I was, and to become that.

I began to live who I was in my mid-thirties, and it has taken me many surprising places. I would not have expected to find myself cruising the Mediterranean on a sailboat, living in Paris, married to an ex-Jesuit priest, following a guru, spending time in India. I didn't expect to have three husbands. I became someone the little girl in me could hardly recognize.

I've lived this mutable life for nearly forty years, enjoying the freedom that the discovery of myself conferred on me. So I'm surprised again, and interested, to learn that my process now has turned to undoing it all. I'm no longer so interested in being who I am. I'm a lot more interested in being less of me, and more of no one. So many of the things I loved have fallen away. In Europe and India I sated myself with travel, and I no longer look at a map with that strong yearning to see what's around the next curve. When I got back to the U.S. from France I discovered that I felt that I had eaten in enough fabulous restaurants and tasted enough exquisite food, and I didn't care what or where I ate any more, as long as it was clean, healthy, and, after a while, vegetarian and organic.

I eased out of my last relationship with a man and into solitary living. It took me a while to learn to wear that costume, but eventually I became very fond of it, and don't think I could ever go back to living with someone else. My opinions are fleeting and changeable, my emotions are rare. Where I used to object to other people projecting their imaginings onto me, I now find that I care very little about it.

I spent all that time and energy in the project of becoming myself, and now in my seventies I find that I'd really rather not be anyone, or, rather, I'll be the understudy. I'll be whoever the drama needs me to be at the time. Of course, I can't be Enrico Caruso or Meryl Streep, but I'll do my best, given my limitations.

This may seem a strange state of being to younger people who are still shaping their lives. It's not an abandonment of life, but rather a recognition of another of life's goals: to be in a state of spiritual connectedness. As a meditator tries to empty his mind, I find in myself the desire to empty my life. It's time to let go of the hard-won me I searched for and nourished and lived with for so many years. I am looking now at eternity on the distant horizon, and I'm not sure how big a bundle I want to be carrying when I get to the gate.

∞ EPILOGUE

I LIVED IN MY COHOUSING COMMUNITY for fifteen years, and gradually my thoughts became reality. Very few people left, and the ones who stayed and the ones who joined us, buying a house or renting space from the residents, became friends. We grew to know each other, and as I predicted, we became close.

In my fifteenth year of living there, at seventy-six, as I was settling in to what I thought would be the rest of my life, my life took another turn in the form of a stroke. At first I couldn't talk, and my right side was paralyzed. I worked hard to come back from it, but after two years of effort I realized that I had recovered all that I was going to. That included much of my speech. Amy told me it was remarkable, but I was frustrated with the gaps in my memory and the halting way I talked. And while my shoulder and hip worked, my right hand and foot remained paralyzed.

I took up residence in a remarkable facility near Jonathan and Lauren, where my physical needs were attended to and the social setting was a lot like the beginnings of my cohousing community. There were approximately sixteen residents. (The number varied with deaths and new residents.) We had been thrown together helter-skelter, and we all knew we'd be there until we died. I settled in, trying at first to regain my strength, and later adopting a routine of reading for hours every day. Gradually the thought crept into my mind that this was a chance to attend to my book. I had written a memoir a couple of years before my stroke. I wrote it as though it were being dictated to me, with hardly a pause to reflect on what came next. When I finished, I hit one of those times where I didn't know what to do next, so I put it away and stopped thinking about it.

Little by little, the book came back into my awareness. I thought that I should finally do something with it. As I was mulling over the form it would take, Amy told me about a couple she had met. They were parents of a daughter in Benjamin's school. They had been in publishing and magazine writing, and had recently opened a business publishing books, called Small Batch Books. It seemed a perfect step to get me through the paralysis that came with the feeling that I didn't know what to do next. They seemed to be a low-key and delightful couple, with an easygoing approach to transforming my written words into a book. I put it in their hands.

I had the feeling that the book was finished, but it needed to be put in order. They read it over and agreed. I left them to their work, and tried not to think about it until I had seen what they did with it. In a few weeks it came back to me, put in order but recognizable as my original writings. They had hardly changed my words, but it was organized in a way that made sense. It gave me distance on my words, which felt strange at first, but gradually I became accustomed to it. Amy had a hand in it, and Trisha Thompson and Fred Levine, my editors, helped me immeasurably.

Now, at seventy-nine, I send it out into the world. It's a package now, complete, and I dedicate it to my family, my editors, and my Guru. ❧

Breinigsville, PA USA
18 December 2010
251739BV00002B/1/P